IVAN TODOROV
KALINA DUROVA
ALEKSANDAR ALEKSANDROV

THE ECONOMY OF BULGARIA: STRUCTURAL FUNDS, GROWTH AND CYCLICAL RECURRENCE

CONTENTS

https://doi.org/10.2478/9783110619218-001

INTRODUCTION

The ability of a nation to ensure improving living standards for its members depends largely on the pace of long-term economic growth. In the long term even seemingly small difference in the rate of economic growth could lead to huge differences in the income of the average citizen. As an economy in transition, Bulgaria is faced with many problems – a heavy structural transformation and a sharp necessity of enhancing competitiveness, of building quality institutions and of increasing productivity. In order to be operational market economy needs not only effective private sector but also quality public institutions, which correct market failures. The privatization process has helped to increase efficiency in resource allocation and reduce the share of public sector in the economy (Stoilova, 2007; Patonov, 2013).

After a heavy financial and economic crisis, in July 1997 Bulgaria introduced a Currency Board Arrangement (CBA), in order to restore the confidence in the national currency and bank system, to impose financial discipline and stabilize the economy. The Bulgarian CBA has proved to be successful. It is a type of a hard currency peg that relies on automatic mechanisms to restore macroeconomic equilibrium, limiting severely the discretion of policymakers (Stoilova, 2010). The state intervention in the economy was restricted, which may be considered "a fundamental precondition for the development of free market economy" (Patonov, 2013).

The CBA adoption in 1997 marked the beginning of a new stage in the economic history of Bulgaria. This stage is characterized by a gradual recovery of Bulgarian economy from the collapse in 1990-s and by an unstable and uneven growth. After a period of a relatively high growth of 6-7% per annum before the global crisis, Bulgarian economy contracted by 5.01 % in 2009 and grew by less than 2% in the next years. The weak growth was accompanied by deflation trends in 2013 and 2014, which is a dangerous combination and requires a rapid and adequate response by Bulgarian macroeconomic policy-makers.

The EU Structural and Cohesion Funds are crucial to a small open economy with a small amount of domestic savings, such as the Bulgarian one, which relies heavily on external financing to finance its investments, generate economic growth and overcome its lagging behind developed European economies. EU cohesion policy has evolved from a purely redistributive mechanism, reflecting primarily the national interests of the member states, to an effective Community instrument for regional development and for economic and social cohesion.

The present research has four objectives:

1. Estimation of the short-term and long-term effects of European funding on the Bulgarian economy;
2. Investigation of the economic growth of Bulgaria in the period of the CBA;
3. Analysis the cyclical recurrence of Bulgaria's economy under a CBA;
4. Formulation of recommendations on macroeconomic policies, which contribute to stimulating growth, to minimizing cyclical fluctuations and to maximizing the benefits of EU funds to Bulgaria.

The goals of the study been achieved through the fulfilment of the following tasks:

- Study of the History and Perspectives of the European Union Cohesion Policy (Chapter one);
- Empirical Analysis of the Impact European Union Cohesion Policy on the Economy of Bulgaria (Chapter one);
- Review of empirical research on Bulgaria's economic growth under the transition to a market-oriented economy (Chapter two);
- Review of the theoretical fundamentals of economic growth (Chapter two);

- Empirical investigation of Bulgaria's short-term and long-term c growth and its drivers on the supply and on the demand side of the economy (Chapter two);
- Review the theoretical foundations of the cyclical recurrence of the economy (Chapter three);
- Empirical estimation of Bulgaria's potential output and cyclical position (Chapter three);
- Empirical Analysis of the main types of markets and their disequilibria;
- Elaboration of variants of macroeconomic policies, which help to stimulate growth, to minimize cyclical fluctuations and to maximize the benefits of EU funds to Bulgaria (Conclusions section).

The study uses the methods of comparative analysis, systematization, theoretical generalization, growth accounting and ordinary least squares (OLS).

https://doi.org/10.2478/9783110619218-002

CHAPTER ONE. THE EUROPEAN UNION COHESION POLICY AND BULGARIA'S ECONOMY

1.1. History and Perspectives of the European Union Cohesion Policy

Manzella and Mendez (2009) explored the evolution of the EU CP in the period 1975-2009. Cohesion policy (CP) has undergone a radical transformation over time. The key dimensions of this transformation can be categorized according to a number of constitutional, financial, strategic and operational dimensions.

Absent in the Treaty of Rome, the CP has strong constitutional foundations nowadays. For the first time, economic and social cohesion was introduced into the Treaty through the Single European Act (SEA) of 1986. It was reaffirmed as the central objective of the EU, together with the Economic and Monetary Union (EMU) and the internal market in the revision of the Maastricht Treaty, of 1993. The Lisbon Treaty added a territorial dimension to the economic and social cohesion, providing a basis for potential expanding the scope of policy towards wider spatial problems, although the exact wording remains controversial (Mirwaldt, McMaster and Bachtler, 2009).

Changes in the constitutional basis of policy coincide with a progressive increase in its financial resources. Since the creation of the European Regional Development Fund (ERDF) in 1975, Cohesion Funds have steadily grown from 5% to 36% of the total EU budget over the period 2007-2013. Although the total share of cohesion funds in the EU GDP is low, they are an important source of economic development resources in poorer EU member states and regions. For example, CP funds received in the period 2000-2006 represent 60% of the total public capital expenditure in Portugal, 48% in Greece and 24% in Spain (European Commission, 2007).

Modifications in the CP are large in both strategic and operational terms. Over time there has been progressive transformation of redistributive mechanism associated with the preferences of the member states to genuine regional development policy. It is based on common EU objectives and priorities and is implemented through an innovative implementation system that includes supranational, national and regional administrations.

For most of CP's history, there has been no comprehensive European strategy to guide its functioning. Various periodic reports and guidelines have been set up by the Commission to assess and guide policy, but only with the reforms of 1999 and 2006 the incorporation of the CP into the EU's Common Strategies has been observed for Economic and Social Development (the European Employment Strategy and the Lisbon Strategy). The Council of Ministers, for the first time, has a role to play in implementing the CPs through the strategic reporting clauses of CP's contribution to the EU objectives in the 2007-2013 period.

As a result of these strategic changes, the aspects of "competitiveness" and "effectiveness" of policy have become increasingly important in recent years, at least in the political debates and documents. For many people, including Commissioners, solidarity and redistribution remain key features of the CP, especially in terms of geographic eligibility and financial intensity of support. Fundamental changes have been observed in the area designation approach, which can be considered a defining feature of regional policy (Bachtler and Mendez, 2007). Since the reforms of 1988, most of the resources have been earmarked for the poorest European regions, which are determined on the basis of criteria and averages for the EU. Previously, all resources were transferred to the member states that spent them on projects within their nationally defined priority areas. Outside less developed regions, the geographic zoning requirements introduced in

1988 and refined in the next two reforms were abolished in the 2007-2013 period by transferring the decisions on the spatial distribution of funds to the member states within the framework of the "Regional Competitiveness and Employment ".

A key innovation in the CP implementation system in 1988 is the creation of a multi-level governance model involving the collective participation of vertical partners (community, national, regional and local authorities) and horizontal stakeholders (business representatives, trade unions, non-governmental organizations, etc.) in the design and implementation of programs in accordance with a common set of organizational and functional criteria and rules. While the organizational and functional systems for designing and implementing the development programs funded by EU differ significantly (as reflecting institutional and cultural differences between and within the member states), the implementation requirements create strong convergence pressures through concepts such as multiannual integrated planning, partnership, monitoring and evaluation, good practices, etc.

Numerous committees, networks, guidelines and activities provide continuous interaction between different levels, resulting in close links between European institutions, national authorities, the private sector and civil society. This contributes to the development of a polycentric transnational administration that shares common values, acts through bodies organized on the basis of the same principles, follows the same procedures and speaks the same technical language. In recent years, the CP has become global through the launch of structured dialogues with non-EU countries (Brazil, China and Russia) and other international organizations (MERCOSUR).

From an evolutionary point of view, CP represents much more than merely redistribution of resources from wealthy member states to the poor ones, although redistribution is still a characteristic of it. The KP has become a powerful regional development tool with the potential to channel resources to achieve EU objectives and to improve administrative practices and culture across Europe.

In its evolution, CP has encountered many problems. One of the recurrent problems is the desire to improve the effectiveness of governance arrangements by seeking an optimal balance between the principle of conditionality (to channel resources for achieving EU objectives) and the principle of subsidiarity (to allow flexibility for the most effective use of the resources). This affects the evolving relationship between the Commission and the member states. For example, in the reforms of 1993 (for the 1994-1999 period), the Commission took a stronger and more active role in negotiating plans and OPs, backed by stronger regulatory requirements for the use of funds. In the next programming period 2000-2006, the responsibility for the key elements of the design and implementation of the programs was delegated to the member states while the Commission extended its influence in monitoring, evaluation and control of the end results with strengthened regulatory requirements in these areas. This trend continued in the 2007-2013 period when the Commission was less involved in the actual implementation of the policy, shifting its focus to audit and control issues the strategic issues with varying degrees of success.

Table 1.1 shows the objectives of EU regional policy for the 2000-2006 and 2007-2013 programming periods. There is no significant difference between them, although there is a further focus on the poorer regions over the period 2007-2013 and most of the cohesion expenditure should be explicitly motivated to help the regions meet the Lisbon criteria for boosting growth, employment and innovation.

The future of EU Cohesion policy has been considered in two reports by the European Committee of the Regions. The first report (European Committee of the Regions, 2015a) outlines the trends and main aspects of effectiveness, efficiency and governance of Cohesion policy from the point of view of local and regional authorities (LRAs). The second report (European Committee of the Regions, 2015b) presents models and ideas for the future of Cohesion policy.

Table 1.1. Comparison between EU regional policy objectives for the 2000-2006 and 2007-2013 programming periods

2000–2006	2007–2013
Objective 1: Regions lagging behind in their development Cohesion fund (money allocated to Spain, Portugal, Greece and Ireland)	Convergence
Objective 2: Economic and social conversion areas Objective 3: Training systems and employment policies Various cohesion programs: Interreg III, URBAN II (financed by the ERDF) и EQUAL (financed by the ESF)	Regional competitiveness and employment European territorial cooperation
Programs based on CAP Leader + EAGGF-Guidance Rural development and restructuring of the fishing sector beyond Objective 1	Second pillar of the CAP

Source: Cohesion Policy 2007-13: Commentaries and Official Texts, January 2007, DG Regio, p. 10.

Regions and places are considered to be key levels in establishing effective coordination of the policies that offer a set of challenges. On the one hand, their capacity to manage the EU's public investment policy is heavily influenced by differences in political and administrative systems in the EU. On the other hand, this capacity is influenced by external economic and social conditions such as demographic challenges, economic downturn in rural areas, population growth, and financial accumulation in growing urban areas.

Closer cooperation between regional and local partners in the member states and their participation in the development and implementation of partnership agreements and operational programs are important in all stages of policy. The strong commitment that offers the opportunity to shape policies and investment priorities according to actual local / regional needs can be ensured through the representation of the managing authorities or the intermediate governing bodies through LRAs. They can assume the role of passive recipients or active policy strategists - the determinant here is the real burden of LRAs in coordinating the different policy approaches formulated by actors at national and local level. The regions managing regional operational programs in countries with a long tradition in regional European structural and investment funds (ESIF) programs (Germany, Spain, France, Italy) benefit from longer-term budgetary commitment to specific development objectives that combine funds from EU, national states and funds at the national level.

On the other hand, in the regions that manage regional operational programs in countries with a decentralization process (Czech Republic, Poland, Slovakia), the stable longer-term financial instruments lead to a decisive change in the capacity for self-government. In these regions, the financing of local infrastructure is gradually being replaced by more innovative and broader types of interventions. This includes all the challenges posed by less developed intermediation whose support in the implementation of programs in developed regions is an important factor for their success.

Coordination of structural funds policy at member state level implies (a) a focus on strategic issues and guidelines to support the speed of policy implementation and (b) lack of communication options and experience for regular exchange of information between operational units. It is useful to involve LRAs in interministerial committees linking the sectoral ministries that coordinate the ESIF at national level to improve the operational management of programs. In countries where such committees don't exist, it is recommended that LRAs be more closely involved in monitoring committees as a coordination mechanism of the ESIF.

The low participation of local authorities in the programming process, as well as their poor representation in partnerships, weakens their management capacity and their capacity to implement the projects. The adaptability of institutions and the process of collective learning are dependent on institutional architecture at national level. This problem can be resolved by assisting member states and different partners in building their own strategies. The focus may be on public innovation policies such as risk assessment training.

From a structural point of view, the project implementation rules need to be simplified and current bureaucracy must be reduced by innovative approaches and improving internal and external communication channels.

The on-site approach favors the mobilization of stakeholders (including the private sector) and their specific territorial expertise. Compatibility between Pan-European overarching goals and territorial realities can be improved (Boehme et al., 2013). The link between political decisions and prospects for people can be enhanced by linking efficiency and democracy, transparency and top-down approaches.

In order to identify the challenges facing each territory and to help define the strategic objectives of a specific region in relation to EU policy, a territorial forecasting approach may be used. The link between cohesion policy funding and sub-national budgets, including the provisions of the Stability Pact, should be clear.

Regarding eligibility to EU funding, the conventions that stimulate regional policy in the member states can become a tool to meet regional needs. It may be useful to create a single

EU mono-fund that supports regions in accordance with their specific needs and challenges.

The implementation of a proportionate audit system, based on a new approach for cooperation and the principle of multi-level governance, needs to be improved. The future evaluation system should be based on more appropriate indicators and effectiveness should be linked to a result-oriented approach.

In terms of accountability, transparency and results orientation, stimulating further exchange of best practices and cases between regions is becoming more and more important.

To overcome the acute economic divide between regions in the EU, the LRA should be adequately involved in the design and implementation of national responses to the strategic framework of the EU for the forthcoming programming period. This will be easy for countries with long tradition of regional self-government, but will pose a significant challenge to some NMS where regional governance is still at an early stage or there is no self-government in the regions. In the latter case, the strategic disruption between national policy goals and local interventions can be even greater. It is necessary that national states and European institutions (in particular the EC's Regional Policy Directorate) provide for proactive guidance in translating strategies into action at local and regional level. New, more pragmatic governance approaches are needed. On the other hand, it is important to show a wider variety of options to local and regional stakeholders in order to avoid the widespread duplication of similar events at the local level (European Committee of the Regions, 2012).

As proposed by Barca (2009), the CP is based on the additionality approach, i.e. it supplements but does not replace the equivalent public expenditure of the member states. Unlike the 2007-2013 programming period, the CP in the current programming period (2014-2020) is in line with the Europe 2020 strategy (through an orientation to 11 thematic objectives drawn from the strategy) and the European semester (by considering country-specific recommendations and the national reform program). The CP is given more attention in the current period due to its specific budget burden (about 32.5% of the EU single policy budget), thematic coverage, spatial orientation, its placement in partner-ship agreements and operational programs and EU reporting requirements (progress reports, strategic report 2017-2019, follow-up policy measures at EU level). CP is not independent, and it comes with tools that are based on sectoral policy implemented by an on-site approach (river basin management plans, research and innovation strategies for smart specialization - RIS3).

Forecasts for the future of CP are of limited value because of the huge number of uncertain internal and external factors. Four scenarios can be outlined, each of which presents possible future situations, influential factors, causal relationships and outcomes (European Committee of the Regions, 2015b):

1. Stability and abundance of resources;
2. Stability and scarcity of resources;
3. Instability and abundance of resources;
4. Instability and scarcity of resources.

Of these scenarios, the third and fourth deserve more attention because of their potential to develop a qualitatively different future CP.

The "Instability and abundance of resources" scenario refers to a situation where there is a relative abundance of resources in an unstable and multipolar world in terms of geopolitics. The market economy fails to deal with its shortcomings and allocate resources efficiently, and the indiscriminate competition for resources will exist at all levels: national, international and local. The financial resources of the CP can be directed to the exploitation of resources and increasing return on investment, ultimately leading to rising inequality and thus undermining its own strategic orientation.

The "Instability and scarcity of resources" scenario: Negative geopolitical development, financial crises and social discontent will be combined with a significant decline in the average standard of living on a global scale. This will lead to a vicious circle of divergent trends in the world's population (migration, urbanization), tension and destabilization at the local level, and a high-risk society. "Cohesion" will become even more important as a policy instrument: it can offer groups of countries / regions (such as the EU) real goals for better coordination and survival. Unlike today's CP, the reason for a future CP will be to optimize the use of scarce resources based on common sense and sound economic logic. The focus on the group of countries regions will shift from trying to prove economic straightness of disputed goals of leaders to achieving a sustainable synergistic state of risk mitigation.

In the "Instability and abundance of resources" scenario, despite the differences between economic and territorial perspectives, policy measures can be summarized as follows:

- Regarding the environment, policy actions are expected to focus on the exploitation of natural resources by investing in infrastructure, although conservation levels may be lower than today's;
- In the labor market, policy measures will follow a model similar to the current CP, but with a stronger emphasis on regulation and control;
- Social policies and health care, although only peripherally involved in the CP, will be influenced by the way in which the infrastructure is provided. Political responses must become more innovative in order to adapt to the changing and seriously fragmented demand;
- Education and closely related research and innovation policies are considered to serve the economic CP. Political responses will have to change, on the one hand, to attract people fleeing from geopolitical instability to education,

research and innovation and, on the other hand, to adapt to the potential and needs of the regions in the sense of research and innovation strategies for smart specialization - RIS3. Geo-political instability will also affect logistics channels and potential markets;

- The transport and energy network and infrastructure and their development will continue to absorb significant resources, but their orientation will change. Political reactions will deviate from their current form and become more specific. Instead of providing basic technical infrastructure, they will have to guarantee multimodal and alternative routes and security;
- In the SME sector and entrepreneurship, policies will need to focus more on the satisfaction of the EU internal market (assuming that stagnation policies will be eased to sustain demand in an aging Europe).

In the "Instability and scarcity of resources" scenario, despite the differences in economic, social and territorial terms, policy measures can be summarized as follows:

- Regarding the environment, policy responses should place a stronger emphasis on the security of resource provision, on eco-efficiency and risk management;
- In the case of labor market policy responses will face major challenges and will have to adjust their goals, instruments and the very concept of what it means inclusion in the labor market;
- Social policies and healthcare will undergo similar changes like those of the labor market. The financial crisis, migration and instability can lead to calls for a reduction in "social services" in order to ease the economy from this "burden". Political responses will have to undergo paradigm shift and invest in sustainability and pro-activity. The forerunner of these changes is the development of childcare in Eastern Europe. The system there is gradually changing from institutionalization to individual voluntary

care in foster families. Public authorities are reluctant to start changes in this area, although empirical studies show higher benefits and lower costs in deinstitutionalized childcare;

- As for education and closely related to its research and innovation, policy responses will need to place greater emphasis on green skills, decentralization and innovation, open innovation and shared use of resources; proprietary approaches and commercialization will weaken;
- The development of transport and energy networks and infrastructure will face a shortage of financial resources. Political responses will have to put a higher priority on investment but at the same time maintain a certain level of connectivity, guaranteeing the Union's functionality;
- In the SME sector and entrepreneurship, political measures will need to focus on satisfying the EU's internal market in conditions of low or no growth; Therefore, SME policy will have to focus on small flexible units that can adapt their production as well as on flexible entrepreneurs. These are micro-enterprises and sole proprietorships, which are considered an indicator of underdeveloped economies these days.

The cost of lack of CP is very different in both scenarios.

Under **the scenario of "Unstableness and abundance of resources"**, assuming the CP will favor temporary alliances and short-term goals, the lack of CP will lead to a slower achievement of these goals as there will be no source of co-financing. This will not change the CP's fundamental model of action.

In **the "Instability and scarcity of resources" scenario**, the CP's role is closer to the original concept. This role will be accentuated by the pressure of insecurity. In the absence of CP, scarce resources and funds will be directed to immediate satisfaction of demand and short-term relief of problems. All intentions of experimentation (an important aspect of CP), innovation, and precautionary management will yield to the reactive preservation of the existing status quo in a vicious circle. Under this scenario, the cost of lack of CP is significant.

The importance of absorbed EU funds for Bulgaria is great for the following reasons:

- EU funds are an important source of financing for investments in Bulgaria, which directly increases capital stock in the Bulgarian economy;
- EU funds contribute to the creation of innovation and raise the technological level of the economy;
- The European Social Fund finances projects that improve the quantity and quality of human capital;
- EU funds finance the construction of important public infrastructure objects that attract foreign investment and stimulate economic growth.

Increasing capital stocks, human capital formation and infrastructure building increase the productive potential, productivity and competitiveness of the Bulgarian economy, which in the long run should raise the standard of living in Bulgaria and help reduce the differences in the development compared to the advanced western European countries.

1.2. Impact of the European Union Cohesion Policy on the Economy of Bulgaria

During the 2007-13 programming period, seven operational programs under the EU Structural and Cohesion Funds (SCF) to the amount of EUR 6.7 billion financed the country's socio-economic development priorities, contributing to narrowing the gap with other EU countries and overcoming the negative effects of the global financial and economic crisis. Bulgaria also received money from the European Agricultural Fund for Rural Development (EAFRD), the European Agricultural Guarantee Fund (EAGF) and the European Fisheries Fund (EFF). By the end of 2015 the progress in the absorption of EU funds in Bulgaria was stable with a contracting ratio of over 100%, a payment ratio of 95% and a European Commission (EC) certification ratio of 81%. While making significant efforts to successfully start the absorption of funds in the new 2014-2020 programming period, the Bulgarian authorities focused on the effective completion of the 2007-2013 period.

The reference period (2015) was characterized by an increasing rate of absorption of EU funds, project budget updates, enhanced monitoring of activities (especially where the risk of delays was high) and a comprehensive review of the causes of delays and adequate prolongation of the deadlines for completion of the projects by the end of 2015. The main challenges were:

- Completion of all projects, including payments until the end of the eligibility period;
- Providing funding for projects that could not be completed by the end of 2015;
- Tackling a huge amount of management verification and suspension of funding under some of the operational programs;
- Preparations for the closure of the 2007-2013 programming period.

Bulgaria's progress in the absorption of EU funds for the period 2007-2015 is summarized in Table 1.2 and the contracting ratio for the separate EU funds is shown in Table 1.3.

Table 1.2. Progress of Bulgaria in the EU funds (ERDF, CF and ESF) absorption for the period 2007-2015

Available budget	6.7 billion EUR
Contracted grants	7.0 billion EUR
Contracting ratio	105%
Paid grants	6.4 billion EUR
Payment ratio	95%
EC certification	5.4 billion EUR
EC certification ratio	81%

Source: Eurostat

Table 1.3. Contracting ratios of Bulgaria for the separate EU funds (ERDF, CF and ESF) for the period 2007-2015

EU fund	Contracting ratio
European Regional Development Fund (ERDF)	106%
Cohesion Fund (CF)	107%
European Social Fund (ESF)	104%

Source: KPMJ (2016). EU Funds in Central and Eastern Europe. Progress Report 2007-2015, p. 23

The implementation of the new programming period 2014-2020 started in 2015 with differences in the level of progress across the different operational programs. By the end of 2015, the contracting ratio was 7.9% and the payment ratio was 0.7%. Bulgaria's progress in the absorption of EU funds for the period 2014-2020 is summarized in Table 1.4.

Table 1.4. Progress of Bulgaria in the EU funds (ERDF, CF and ESF) absorption for the period 2014-2020

Available budget	7.3 billion EUR
Contracted grants	0.58 billion EUR
Contracting ratio	7.92%
Paid grants	0.054 billion EUR
Payment ratio	0.70%
EC certification	0.003 billion EUR
EC certification ratio	0.04%

Source: https://eumis2020.government.bg/

In Bulgaria there was a trend of accelerated absorption of the European funds and of precise planning of the projects. The analyzed period 2007-2015 was characterized by:

- Contracting more funds than the available budget under some operational programs in order to manage the financial risk at the end of the programming period;
- Activities that could not be finalized by the end of 2015 remained at the expense of the beneficiary;
- Increased attention to the quality of control at central and regional level.

Bulgaria put a lot of efforts into the successful completion of its first programming period under the EU SCF. The structuring and implementation of financial engineering tools was considered a good practice in Bulgaria. Some of the major infrastructure projects were successfully completed, such as the Sofia Metro, which is among the 30 most extensive metro systems in Europe. The extension of Metro Line 1 to Sofia Airport was officially opened in 2015. The other extensions were launched and prepared for further investment. The development of the Unified Management Information System for the EU Structural Instruments in Bulgaria continued in order to improve its functionality and to facilitate the management and control of the EU funds in the previous and the new programming period.

The main problems of the management of the European funds in Bulgaria are:

- Irregularities in public procurements which led to suspension of funding and financial corrections under some operational programs;
- Lack of working capital, which directly affects the pace of progress and the quality of implementation;
- Insufficient exchange of knowledge and experience between managing authorities, beneficiaries and control bodies.

The following lessons can be drawn from the management and absorption of EU funds in Bulgaria for the period 2007-2013:

- It is advisable that the implementation of projects for the new programming period 2014-2020 start as soon as possible;
- Adopt a new approach in the OP Regions for Growth 2014-2020 in order to avoid concentrating funds in major cities, which was typical for the 2007-2013 period;
- Digitalization of the project application process for the new programming period;
- Codification of the legislation on European funds, which led to the adoption of the European Structural and Investment Funds Management Act at the end of 2015.

Empirical analysis of the short-term effects of the EU funds on economic growth, employment and unemployment in Bulgaria

Methodology

The methodology used in this study is an OLS analysis of time series data. The following equations were estimated

(1.1) $GDPGR_t = a_0 + a_1*GDPGR_t(-1) + a_2*EUFAR_t + a_3*ESI_t + a_4*EUAVGDPGR_t + a_5*EUFGDP_t + u_t$

(1.2) $EMPLR_t = b_0 + b_1*EMPLR_t(-1) + b_2*EUFAR_t + b_3*ESI_t + a_4*EUAVGDPGR_t + a_5*EUFGDP_t + u_t$

(1.3) $UNEMPLR_t = c_0 + c_1*UNEMPLR_t(-1) + c_2*EUFAR_t + c_3*ESI_t + c_4*EUAVGDPGR_t + c_5*EUFGDP_t + u_t$

where: $\mathbf{GDPGR_t}$ - real GDP growth rate of Bulgaria in quarter **t** compared to the previous quarter **t-1**; $\mathbf{EMPLR_t}$ - employment rate in Bulgaria in quarter **t**; $\mathbf{UNEMPLR_t}$ - rate of unemployment in Bulgaria in quarter **t**; $\mathbf{EUFAR_t}$ - rate of absorption of the ERDF, CF and ESF funds in Bulgaria in quarter **t**; $\mathbf{ESI_t}$ - economic sentiment indicator in Bulgaria in quarter **t**; $\mathbf{EUAVGDPGR_t}$ - average real GDP growth in the EU in quarter **t**; $\mathbf{EUFGDP_t}$ - ratio of the absorbed EU funds to the real GDP of Bulgaria in quarter **t**; $\mathbf{a_0, b_0, c_0}$ - intercepts; $\mathbf{a_1, a_2, a_3, a_4, a_5, b_1, b_2, b_3, b_4, b_5, c_1, c_2, c_3, c_4, c_5}$ - regression coefficients; $\mathbf{u_t}$ – error term.

Equations (1.1), (1.2) and (1.3) include a set of control variables to take into account various effects related to the international economic environment and the economic situation in Bulgaria (see Table 1.5). The variable that is of interest in this study is the rate of absorption of EU funds.

Table 1.5. Description of independent variables in Equations (1.1), (1.2) and (1.3)

Independent variables	Explanation	Expected sign
EUFAR	The rate of absorption of the ERDF, CF and ESF funds is calculated as a ratio of the paid grants for the respective quarter to the available budget of Bulgaria for the 2007-2013 programming period. Positive signs of this variable are expected in the equations for economic growth and employment, but a negative sign in the equation for unemployment since countries with a better administrative capacity can attract more funds to support their economic recovery.	Positive (+) in Equations (1.1) and (1.2) Negative (-) in Equation (1.3)

ESI	Economic sentiment indicator, calculated by the EC for each member state. When **ESI** rises, the general perception of investors about the economic situation improve. Low levels of this indicator have a detrimental impact on investment and consumption and impede economic recovery.	Positive (+) in Equations (1.1) and (1.2) Negative (-) in Equation (1.3)
EUAVGDPGR	Average growth rate of real GDP in the EU compared to the previous quarter. This indicator reflects the general economic situation in the EU and is associated with the international economic perspectives.	Positive (+) in Equations (1.1) and (1.2) Negative (-) in Equation (1.3)
EUFGDP	A ratio of the absorbed EU funds to real GDP, which can be associated with the macroeconomic absorption capacity.	Positive (+) in Equations (1.1) and (1.2) Negative (-) in Equation (1.3)

Source: Prepared by the author

Data

The data for the calculations of the indicators in this study were extracted from the website https://www.eufunds.bg/izpalnenie-na-operativnite-programi and from Eurostat. Monthly and quarterly data for the 2010-2015 period were used. The monthly data (for **EUFAR** and **ESI**) were averaged and transformed into quarterly. The investigation period (2010-2015) differs from the programming period (2007-2013), as the actual disbursement of funds over the 2007-2013 programming period began in 2008 and ended in 2015, but monthly data on the absorption of the EU funds from Bulgaria are available from the beginning of 2010.

The descriptive statistics of the variables in Equations (1.1), (1.2) and (1.3) are shown in Table 1.6. In the period 2010-2015 the economic growth in Bulgaria varied from -1.10% to 6.00% and had an average of 2.03%. The average economic growth in the EU ranged from -1.6% to 4.10%, with an average of 1.29%. The quarterly absorption of EU funds in Bulgaria ranged from -0.82% to 9.52%, with an average of 3.22%. The economic sentiment indicator had a minimum of 89.23 and a maximum of 104.90 and its average value was 96.65. The employment rate ranged from 65.60% to 69.30% and had an average of 67.72%. The unemployment rate ranged from 8.10% to 13.10% and had an average of 11.23%. The ratio of the absorbed EU funds to real GDP had a minimum of -1.60%, a maximum of 4.10% and an average of 1.29%.

Table 1.6. Descriptive statistics of the variables in Equations (1.1), (1.2) and (1.3)

	GDPGR, %	EMPLR, %	UNEMPLR, %	EUFAR, %	ESI	EUAVGDPGR, %	EUFGDP, %
Mean	2.03	67.72	11.23	3.22	96.68	1.29	2.17
Maximum	6.00	69.30	13.10	9.52	104.90	4.10	6.51
Minimum	-1.10	65.60	8.10	-0.82	89.23	-1.60	-0.56
Standard deviation	2.01	1.31	1.37	2.34	4.26	1.39	1.57
Number of observations	24	24	24	24	24	24	24

Source: Prepared by the author

The analysis of time series data continued with group tests for stationarity (see Table 1.7). The results of the stationarity tests showed that the alternative hypothesis of the absence of a unit root and of the stationarity of the variables should be accepted at a significance level of 5%.

Table 1.7. Group unit root tests of the variables in Equations (1.1), (1.2) and (1.3)

Type of test	Probability
Im, Pesaran and Shin W-stat	0.01
ADF - Fisher Chi-square	0.00
PP - Fisher Chi-square	0.00

Source: Prepared by the author

Results

The results of the OLS estimation of Equation (1.1) are shown in Table 1.8.

Table 1.8. Estimates of the coefficients in Equation (1.1) for the period 2010-2015

Variable	Coefficient	Standard error	t-statistic	Probability
Constant	3.21	9.34	0.34	0.74
GDPGR(-1)	0.33	0.22	1.47	0.16
EUFAR	4.60	4.60	1.00	0.33
ESI	-0.03	0.10	-0.31	0.76
EUAVGDPGR	0.60	0.31	1.92	0.07
EUFGDP	-6.75	6.85	-0.99	0.34

Source: Prepared by the author

Only the average EU growth rate **EUAVGDPGR** (significant at a level of 10%) affected the short-term economic growth of Bulgaria **GDPGR** over the period 2010-2015. The other variables in the model are not significant.

The regression coefficient before **EUAVGDPGR** is positive and corresponds to theoretical expectations. Its value (0.60) shows that a 1% change in the rate of average economic growth in the EU will lead to 0.60% change in the rate of economic growth in Bulgaria in the same direction provided that other variables are held constant.

The value of the coefficient of determination (0.64) shows that 64% of the changes in Bulgaria's short-term economic growth rate can be explained by changes in the international economic conjuncture. The probability of the F-statistic (0.00) indicates that the alternative hypothesis of adequacy of the model used is confirmed at a significance level of 5%. The acceptance of the alternative hypothesis does not mean that the model specification is the best possible but only that the regression model adequately reflects the relationship between dependent variable and independent variables.

The value of 2.54 of the Durbin-Watson statistic presumes the existence of serial correlation (autocorrelation) of residuals. The LM serial correlation test (see Table 1.9) confirmed the alternative hypothesis of a serial correlation at a significance level of 5%. The serial correlation of residuals is not unusual for time-series data. In the presence of serial correlation OLS estimates and based on them forecasts are inefficient but still unbiased and consistent. Since the regression model will not be used for forecasting, the serial correlation was not removed from the model.

Table 1.9. Serial correlation LM test on the residuals of Equation (1.1)

Breusch-Godfrey Serial Correlation LM Test:				
F-statistic	5.443854	Prob. F(2,15)		0.0167
Obs*R-squared	9.673211	Prob. Chi-Square(2)		0.0079
Test Equation:				
Dependent Variable: RESID				
Method: Least Squares				
Date: 05/19/17 Time: 15:21				
Sample: 2010Q2 2015Q4				
Included observations: 23				
Presample missing value lagged residuals set to zero.				
Variable	Coefficient	Std. Error	t-Statistic	Prob.
C	1.052616	7.860435	0.133913	0.8953
GDPGR(-1)	0.396499	0.230960	1.716740	0.1066
EUFAR	-2.085114	4.037181	-0.516478	0.6131
ESI	-0.023231	0.080775	-0.287607	0.7776
EUAVGDPGR	-0.064797	0.266927	-0.242752	0.8115
EUFGDP	3.282282	6.018084	0.545403	0.5935
RESID(-1)	-0.961628	0.308716	-3.114930	0.0071
RESID(-2)	-0.599637	0.248260	-2.415355	0.0289
R-squared	0.420574	Mean dependent var		-3.86E-16
Adjusted R-squared	0.150176	S.D. dependent var		1.157462
S.E. of regression	1.067017	Akaike info criterion		3.235819
Sum squared resid	17.07789	Schwarz criterion		3.630774
Log likelihood	-29.21192	Hannan-Quinn criter.		3.335149
F-statistic	1.555387	Durbin-Watson stat		1.744626
Prob(F-statistic)	0.223273			

Source: Prepared by the author

The residual heteroscedasticity test (ARCH) confirmed the null hypothesis of the absence of heteroscedasticity at the 5% level of significance (see Table 1.10).

Table 1.10. Heteroscedasticity test (ARCH) on the residuals of Equation (1.1)

Heteroscedasticity Test: ARCH				
F-statistic	2.014205	Prob. F(1,20)		0.1712
Obs*R-squared	2.012905	Prob. Chi-Square(1)		0.1560
Test Equation:				
Dependent Variable: RESID^2				
Method: Least Squares				
Date: 05/19/17 Time: 15:31				
Sample (adjusted): 2010Q3 2015Q4				
Included observations: 22 after adjustments				
Variable	Coefficient	Std. Error	t-Statistic	Prob.
C	0.860574	0.375989	2.288827	0.0331
RESID^2(-1)	0.301780	0.212637	1.419227	0.1712
R-squared	0.091496	Mean dependent var		1.253865
Adjusted R-squared	0.046070	S.D. dependent var		1.220346
S.E. of regression	1.191904	Akaike info criterion		3.275489
Sum squared resid	28.41269	Schwarz criterion		3.374674
Log likelihood	-34.03037	Hannan-Quinn criter.		3.298854
F-statistic	2.014205	Durbin-Watson stat		1.609530
Prob(F-statistic)	0.171231			

Source: Prepared by the author

The residual normality test (Jarque-Bera) confirmed the null hypothesis of the presence of normal distribution of residuals at the 5% level of significance (see Figure 1.1).

Figure 1.1. Histogram of the residuals of Equation (1.1)

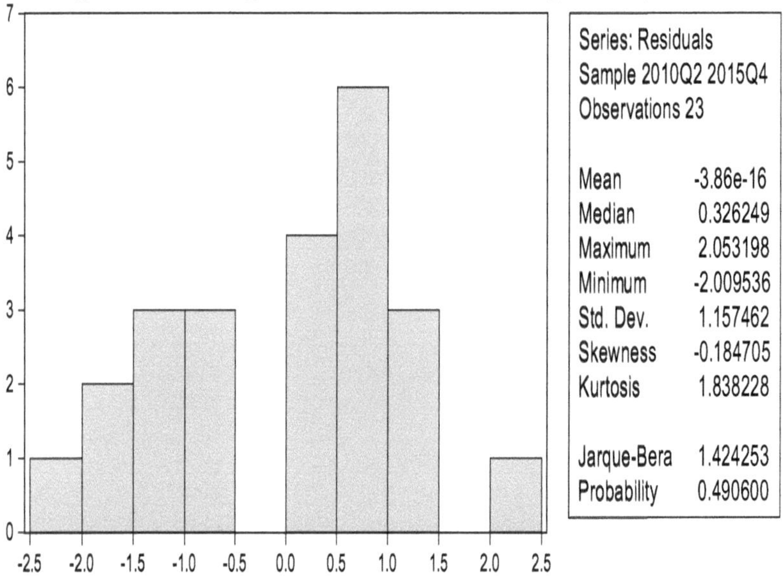

Source: Prepared by the author

Ramsey's Regression Specification Error Test (RESET) confirmed the null hypothesis of the absence of errors in the specification of the regression model (see Table 1.11.).

Table 1.11. Regression Specification Error Test on Equation (1.1)

Ramsey RESET Test				
Equation: EQ_EC_GR				
Specification: GDPGR C GDPGR(-1) EUFAR ESI EUAVGDPGR				
EUFGDP				
Omitted Variables: Squares of fitted values				
	Value	df	Probability	
t-statistic	1.343591	16	0.1978	
F-statistic	1.805238	(1, 16)	0.1978	
Likelihood ratio	2.458791	1	0.1169	
F-test summary:				
	Sum of Sq.	df	Mean Squares	
Test SSR	2.988292	1	2.988292	
Restricted SSR	29.47382	17	1.733754	
Unrestricted SSR	26.48553	16	1.655346	
Unrestricted SSR	26.48553	16	1.655346	
LR test summary:				
	Value	df		
Restricted LogL	-35.48768	17		
Unrestricted LogL	-34.25829	16		
Unrestricted Test Equation:				
Dependent Variable: GDPGR				
Method: Least Squares				
Date: 05/19/17 Time: 15:52				
Sample: 2010Q2 2015Q4				
Included observations: 23				
Variable	Coefficient	Std. Error	t-Statistic	Prob.
C	-7.597932	12.16562	-0.624541	0.5411
GDPGR(-1)	0.076571	0.285888	0.267837	0.7922
EUFAR	-2.813861	7.114231	-0.395526	0.6977
ESI	0.079708	0.124037	0.642617	0.5296
EUAVGDPGR	0.214250	0.419201	0.511091	0.6163
EUFGDP	4.236961	10.56693	0.400964	0.6938
FITTED^2	0.204946	0.152536	1.343591	0.1978
R-squared	0.675654	Mean dependent var		1.891304
Adjusted R-squared	0.554024	S.D. dependent var		1.926587
S.E. of regression	1.286602	Akaike info criterion		3.587677
Sum squared resid	26.48553	Schwarz criterion		3.933262
Log likelihood	-34.25829	Hannan-Quinn criter.		3.674591
F-statistic	5.555006	Durbin-Watson stat		2.641311
Prob(F-statistic)	0.002797			

Source: Prepared by the author

The results of OLS estimation of Equation (1.2) are shown in Table 1.12.

Table 1.12. Estimates of the coefficients in Equation (1.2) for the period 2010-2015

Variable	Coefficient	Standard error	t-statistic	Probability
Constant	-3.31	5.77	-0.57	0.57
EMPLR(-1)	1.06	0.10	10.90	0.00
EUFAR	-0.77	1.28	-0.60	0.56
ESI	-0.00	0.03	-0.16	0.88
EUAVGDPGR	-0.06	0.06	-0.97	0.34
EUFGDP	1.11	1.91	0.58	0.57

Source: Prepared by the author

The employment rate in Bulgaria for the period 2010-2015 **EMPLR** was influenced only by the employment rate in the previous quarter **EMPLR(-1)**, which is significant at a level of 1%. The other independent variables are not significant and did not affect the employment rate.

The coefficient before **EMPLR(-1)** is positive and corresponds to theoretical expectations. Its value of 1.06 shows that 1% change in the employment rate in Bulgaria in the previous quarter will lead, if other factors remain unchanged, to 1.06% change in the employment rate in the current quarter in the same direction.

The value of the coefficient of determination (0.92) shows that 92% of the changes in the employment rate in Bulgaria can be explained by the changes in the rate of employment in the previous period. The probability of the F-statistic (0.00) indicates that the alternative hypothesis of adequacy of the model used is confirmed at a level of significance of 5%. The acceptance of the alternative hypothesis does not mean that the model specification is the best possible but only that the regression model adequately reflects the relationship between dependent variable and independent variables.

The value of 2.14 of the Durbin-Watson statistic presumes the lack of serial correlation (autocorrelation) of residuals. At the 5% level of significance the serial correlation LM test confirmed the null hypothesis that residuals are not serially correlated (see Table 1.13).

Table 1.13 Serial correlation LM test on the residuals of Equation (1.2)

Breusch-Godfrey Serial Correlation LM Test:				
F-statistic	0.067195	Prob. F(2,15)		0.9353
Obs*R-squared	0.204236	Prob. Chi-Square(2)		0.9029
Test Equation:				
Dependent Variable: RESID				
Method: Least Squares				
Date: 05/19/17 Time: 16:17				
Sample: 2010Q2 2015Q4				
Included observations: 23				
Presample missing value lagged residuals set to zero.				
Variable	Coefficient	Std. Error	t-Statistic	Prob.
C	-0.831923	7.256139	-0.114651	0.9102
EMPLR(-1)	0.019440	0.126503	0.153670	0.8799
EUFAR	0.092424	1.445122	0.063956	0.9498
ESI	-0.004813	0.033730	-0.142681	0.8884
EUAVGDPGR	-0.007713	0.070121	-0.109993	0.9139
EUFGDP	-0.139681	2.144741	-0.065127	0.9489
RESID(-1)	-0.112416	0.308057	-0.364918	0.7203
RESID(-2)	-0.015015	0.298658	-0.050275	0.9606
R-squared	0.008880	Mean dependent var		1.35E-14
Adjusted R-squared	-0.453643	S.D. dependent var		0.325499
S.E. of regression	0.392444	Akaike info criterion		1.235364
Sum squared resid	2.310188	Schwarz criterion		1.630318
Log likelihood	-6.206683	Hannan-Quinn criter.		1.334694
F-statistic	0.019199	Durbin-Watson stat		2.008325
Prob(F-statistic)	0.999989			

Source: Prepared by the author

The results of the residual heteroscedasticity test (see Table 1.14) give reason to accept the zero hypothesis of lack of heteroscedasticity in Equation (1.2).

Table 1.14 Heteroscedasticity test (ARCH) on the residuals of Equation (1.2)

Heteroscedasticity Test: ARCH				
F-statistic	0.049956	Prob. F(1,20)		0.8254
Obs*R-squared	0.054814	Prob. Chi-Square(1)		0.8149
Test Equation:				
Dependent Variable: RESID^2				
Method: Least Squares				
Date: 05/19/17 Time: 16:25				
Sample (adjusted): 2010Q3 2015Q4				
Included observations: 22 after adjustments				
Variable	Coefficient	Std. Error	t-Statistic	Prob.
C	0.110612	0.041086	2.692219	0.0140
RESID^2(-1)	-0.049746	0.222570	-0.223508	0.8254
R-squared	0.002492	Mean dependent var		0.105415
Adjusted R-squared	-0.047384	S.D. dependent var		0.155246
S.E. of regression	0.158881	Akaike info criterion		-0.754811
Sum squared resid	0.504865	Schwarz criterion		-0.655626
Log likelihood	10.30292	Hannan-Quinn criter.		-0.731446
F-statistic	0.049956	Durbin-Watson stat		1.873693
Prob(F-statistic)	0.825407			

Source: Prepared by the author

The requirement of normal residual distribution is observed in Equation (1.2) (see Figure 1.2). The probability of the Jarque-Bera statistics is 0.39, which gives reason to accept the zero hypothesis of a normal distribution of the residuals.

Figure 1.2 Histogram of the residuals of Equation (1.2)

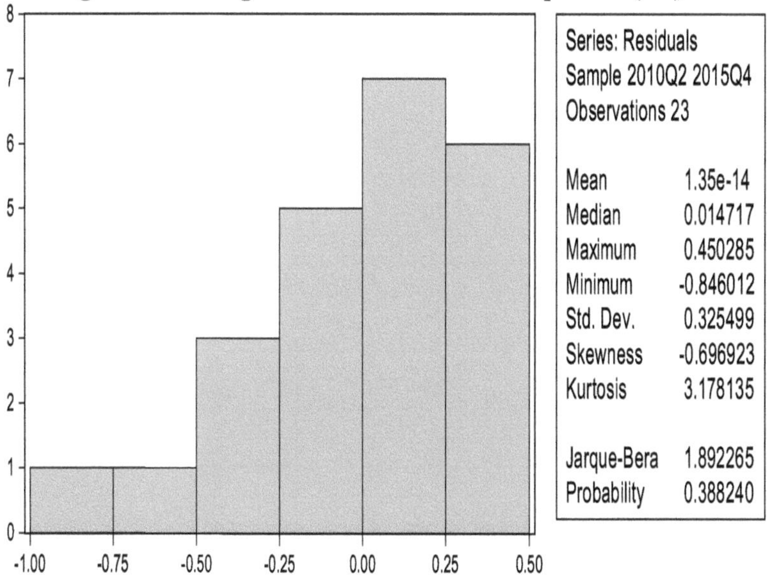

Source: Prepared by the author

The Ramsey's RESET Test confirmed the zero hypothesis of the lack of errors in the specification of Equation (1.2) (see Table 1.15).

Table 1.15. Regression Specification Error Test on Equation (1.2)

Ramsey RESET Test				
Equation: EQ_EMPL				
Specification: EMPLR C EMPLR(-1) EUFAR ESI EUAVGDPGR				
EUFGDP				
Omitted Variables: Squares of fitted values				
	Value	df	Probability	
t-statistic	0.282337	16	0.7813	
F-statistic	0.079714	(1, 16)	0.7813	
Likelihood ratio	0.114305	1	0.7353	
F-test summary:				
	Sum of Sq.	df	Mean Squares	
Test SSR	0.011555	1	0.011555	
Restricted SSR	2.330885	17	0.137111	
Unrestricted SSR	2.319330	16	0.144958	
Unrestricted SSR	2.319330	16	0.144958	
LR test summary:				
	Value	df		
Restricted LogL	-6.309257	17		
Unrestricted LogL	-6.252105	16		
Unrestricted Test Equation:				
Dependent Variable: EMPLR				
Method: Least Squares				
Date: 05/19/17 Time: 16:35				
Sample: 2010Q2 2015Q4				
Included observations: 23				
Variable	Coefficient	Std. Error	t-Statistic	Prob.
C	-144.0335	498.4765	-0.288948	0.7763
EMPLR(-1)	5.075581	14.22557	0.356793	0.7259
EUFAR	-3.554716	9.959791	-0.356907	0.7258
ESI	-0.017923	0.055750	-0.321482	0.7520
EUAVGDPGR	-0.286375	0.804200	-0.356099	0.7264
EUFGDP	5.147208	14.42474	0.356832	0.7259
FITTED^2	-0.028119	0.099595	-0.282337	0.7813
R-squared	0.939171	Mean dependent var		67.76957
Adjusted R-squared	0.916360	S.D. dependent var		1.316481
S.E. of regression	0.380734	Akaike info criterion		1.152357
Sum squared resid	2.319330	Schwarz criterion		1.497942
Log likelihood	-6.252105	Hannan-Quinn criter.		1.239271
F-statistic	41.17208	Durbin-Watson stat		2.130915
Prob(F-statistic)	0.000000			

Source: Prepared by the author

The results of the OLS estimation of Equation (1.3) are shown in Table 1.16.

Table 1.16 Estimates of the coefficients in Equation (1.3) for the period 2010-2015

Variable	Coefficient	Standard error	t-statistics	Probability
Constant	10.10	2.83	3.56	0.00
UNEMPLR(-1)	0.86	0.08	10.25	0.00
EUFAR	-1.07	1.36	-0.78	0.44
ESI	-0.09	0.03	-3.19	0.01
EUAVGDPGR	-0.08	0.07	-1.24	0.23
EUFGDP	1.60	2.04	0.78	0.44

Source: Prepared by the author

During the period 2010-2015 the rate of unemployment in Bulgaria **UNEMPLR** was influenced by the rate of unemployment in the previous quarter **UNEMPLR(-1)** and by the expectations of economic agents **ESI**, which are significant at a level of 5%. The other variables in the model are not significant.

The signs of significant regression coefficients are positive before **UNEMPLR(-1)** and negative before **ESI**, which corresponds to theoretical expectations. The value of the coefficient before **UNEMPLR(-1)** of 0.86 means that a 1% change in the unemployment rate in Bulgaria in the previous quarter, with other factors held constant, results in a 0.86% change in the unemployment rate in the current quarter in the same direction. The value of the coefficient before **ESI** of -0.09 indicates that, if other variables remain constant, a change in **ESI** with one unit causes a 0.09% change in the unemployment rate in the opposite direction.

The value of the coefficient of determination (0.93) shows that 93% of the changes in the unemployment rate in Bulgaria can be explained by the changes in the attitudes of the economic agents and the unemployment rate in the previous period. The probability of the F-statistic (0.00) indicates that the alternative hypothesis for the adequacy of the regression model is accepted. The acceptance of the alternative hypothesis does not mean that the model specification is the best possible but only that the regression model adequately reflects the relationship between dependent variable and independent variables.

The serial correlation LM test (see Table 1.17) confirmed the zero hypothesis of a lack of serial correlation at a significance level of 5%.

Table 1.17. Serial correlation LM test on the residuals of Equation (1.3)

Breusch-Godfrey Serial Correlation LM Test:				
F-statistic	3.076777	Prob. F(2,15)		0.0759
Obs*R-squared	6.690684	Prob. Chi-Square(2)		0.0352
Test Equation:				
Dependent Variable: RESID				
Method: Least Squares				
Date: 05/19/17 Time: 17:09				
Sample: 2010Q2 2015Q4				
Included observations: 23				
Presample missing value lagged residuals set to zero.				
Variable	Coefficient	Std. Error	t-Statistic	Prob.
C	-1.190257	2.607763	-0.456428	0.6546
UNEMPLR(-1)	0.046010	0.079850	0.576200	0.5730
EUFAR	-0.276747	1.292301	-0.214150	0.8333
ESI	0.007780	0.025559	0.304391	0.7650
EUAVGDPGR	0.006600	0.060182	0.109661	0.9141
EUFGDP	0.374816	1.926476	0.194560	0.8483
RESID(-1)	-0.543265	0.250838	-2.165797	0.0468
RESID(-2)	-0.489226	0.259315	-1.886613	0.0787
R-squared	0.290899	Mean dependent var		-5.48E-15
Adjusted R-squared	-0.040014	S.D. dependent var		0.345249
S.E. of regression	0.352088	Akaike info criterion		1.018339
Sum squared resid	1.859493	Schwarz criterion		1.413293
Log likelihood	-3.710896	Hannan-Quinn criter.		1.117669
F-statistic	0.879079	Durbin-Watson stat		2.187803
Prob(F-statistic)	0.545116			

Source: Prepared by the author

The residual heteroscedasticity test (see Table 1.18) confirmed the null hypothesis of the absence of heteroscedasticity in Equation (1.3).

Table 1.18. Heteroscedasticity test (ARCH) on the residuals of Equation (1.3)

Heteroscedasticity Test: ARCH				
F-statistic	0.582495	Prob. F(1,20)		0.4542
Obs*R-squared	0.622611	Prob. Chi-Square(1)		0.4301
Test Equation:				
Dependent Variable: RESID^2				
Method: Least Squares				
Date: 05/19/17 Time: 17:17				
Sample (adjusted): 2010Q3 2015Q4				
Included observations: 22 after adjustments				
Variable	Coefficient	Std. Error	t-Statistic	Prob.
C	0.099524	0.057345	1.735529	0.0980
RESID^2(-1)	0.167657	0.219672	0.763214	0.4542
R-squared	0.028301	Mean dependent var		0.119189
Adjusted R-squared	-0.020284	S.D. dependent var		0.237890
S.E. of regression	0.240291	Akaike info criterion		0.072575
Sum squared resid	1.154795	Schwarz criterion		0.171761
Log likelihood	1.201671	Hannan-Quinn criter.		0.095940
F-statistic	0.582495	Durbin-Watson stat		1.826235
Prob(F-statistic)	0.454245			

Source: Prepared by the author

The requirement of normal residual distribution is observed in Equation (1.3) (see Figure 1.3). The probability of the Jarque-Bera statistics is 0.015, which gives reason to accept the zero hypothesis of a normal residual distribution at a critical level of significance of 1%.

Figure 1.3. Histogram of the residuals of Equation (1.3)

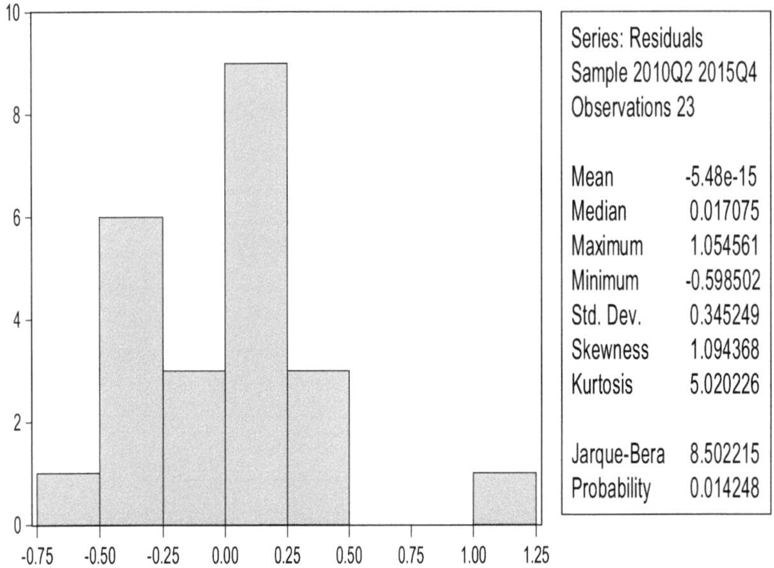

Source: Prepared by the author

The Ramsey's RESET Test confirmed the zero hypothesis of the lack of errors in the specification of Equation (1.3) (see Table 1.19).

Table 1.19. Regression Specification Error Test on Equation (1.3)

Ramsey RESET Test				
Equation: EQ_UNEMPL				
Specification: UNEMPLR C UNEMPLR(-1) EUFAR ESI EUAVGDPGR				
EUFGDP				
Omitted Variables: Squares of fitted values				
	Value	df	Probability	
t-statistic	0.092203	16	0.9277	
F-statistic	0.008501	(1, 16)	0.9277	
Likelihood ratio	0.012217	1	0.9120	
F-test summary:				
	Sum of Sq.	df	Mean Squares	

Test SSR	0.001393	1	0.001393	
Restricted SSR	2.622325	17	0.154254	
Unrestricted SSR	2.620933	16	0.163808	
Unrestricted SSR	2.620933	16	0.163808	
LR test summary:				
	Value	df		
Restricted LogL	-7.664110	17		
Unrestricted LogL	-7.658001	16		
Unrestricted Test Equation:				
Dependent Variable: UNEMPLR				
Method: Least Squares				
Date: 05/19/17 Time: 17:27				
Sample: 2010Q2 2015Q4				
Included observations: 23				
Variable	Coefficient	Std. Error	t-Statistic	Prob.
C	10.49104	5.156274	2.034617	0.0588
UNEMPLR(-1)	0.949684	0.974488	0.974547	0.3443
EUFAR	-1.197132	1.986355	-0.602678	0.5552
ESI	-0.095692	0.092341	-1.036281	0.3155
EUAVGDPGR	-0.090637	0.120536	-0.751954	0.4630
EUFGDP	1.791839	2.968375	0.603643	0.5545
FITTED^2	-0.004750	0.051521	-0.092203	0.9277
R-squared	0.933730	Mean dependent var		11.30435
Adjusted R-squared	0.908879	S.D. dependent var		1.340786
S.E. of regression	0.404732	Akaike info criterion		1.274609
Sum squared resid	2.620933	Schwarz criterion		1.620194
Log likelihood	-7.658001	Hannan-Quinn criter.		1.361522
F-statistic	37.57302	Durbin-Watson stat		2.641182
Prob(F-statistic)	0.000000			

Source: Prepared by the author

Empirical assessment of the impact of the absorption of EU funds on the natural rate of unemployment and the rate of long-term unemployment

Assumptions and methodology

It is assumed that in the long run all markets in the economy (labor, goods and money) are in a balanced state, with real GDP being equal to the potential, and the actual unemployment rate equal to the natural rate of unemployment. The natural rate of unemployment is a sum of the rates of structural and frictional unemployment (Todorov, 2017):

(1.4) NRU = SUR + FUR

where **NRU** is the natural rate of unemployment, **SUR** - the rate of structural unemployment, **FUR** - the rate of frictional unemployment.

As an approximation for the structural unemployment rate **SUR**, the long-term unemployment rate **LTUR** can be used:

(1.5) SUR = LTUR

The long-term unemployment rate **LTUR** is the percentage share of the long-term unemployed (those who have been unemployed for at least one year) **LTU** in the labor force **LF**:

(1.6) LTUR = (LTU / LF) * 100%

The rate of frictional unemployment **FUR** results from labor migration and is assumed to be zero in the long run. Hence, in the long term the natural rate of unemployment **NRU** can be considered equal to the long-term unemployment rate **LTUR**:

(1.7) NRU = LTUR

The impact of the rate of absorption of EU funds on the rate of long-term unemployment (the natural rate of unemployment) was estimated by the equation

(1.8) $\mathbf{LTUR_t = d_0 + d_1{*}EUFAR_t + d_2{*}GDPGR_t + u_t}$

where: $\mathbf{LTUR_t}$ - the long-term unemployment rate in Bulgaria in quarter **t**; $\mathbf{EUFAR_t}$ - rate of absorption of the ERDF, CF and ESF in Bulgaria in quarter **t**; $\mathbf{GDPGR_t}$ - growth rate of Bulgaria's real GDP in quarter **t** compared to the previous quarter **t-1**; $\mathbf{d_0}$ – constant (intercept); $\mathbf{d_1}$, $\mathbf{d_2}$ - regression coefficients; $\mathbf{u_t}$ – error term.

The methodology used was an OLS regression of time series.

Data

Quarterly data of the National Statistical Institute (NSI) on the long-term unemployment rate **LTUR** (in the 15-64 age group) and on the real GDP growth rate **GDPGR** as well as monthly data from the website https://www.eufunds.bg/ on the rate of absorption of EU funds **EUFAR** for the period 2010-2015 were employed. The monthly data for the rate of absorption of EU funds were averaged over quarters and transformed into quarterly.

Quarterly absorption of EU funds in Bulgaria ranged from -0.82% to 9.52%, with an average of 3.22%. The long-term unemployment rate in Bulgaria had a minimum of 4.21% and a maximum of 7.89% and its average value was 6.33%. In the period 2010-2015, economic growth in Bulgaria varied from -1.10% to 6.00% and was 2.03% on average (see Table 1.20).

Table 1.20 Descriptive statistics of the variables in Equation (1.8)

	LTUR, %	EUFAR, %	GDPGR, %
Mean	6.33	3.22	2.03
Maximum	7.89	9.52	6.00
Minimum	4.21	-0.82	-1.10
Standard deviation	1.03	2.34	2.01
Number of observations	24	24	24

Source: Prepared by the author

The analysis of time series data proceeded with group stationarity tests (see Table 1.21). The results of the stationarity tests indicated that there is a reason to accept the alternative hypothesis of the absence of a unit root and of the stationarity of the variables.

Table 1.21. Group unit root tests for the variables in Equation (1.8)

Type of test	Probability
Levin, Lin & Chu t	0.04
Im, Pesaran and Shin W-stat	0.00
ADF - Fisher Chi-square	0.00
PP - Fisher Chi-square	0.00

Source: Prepared by the author

Results

The results from the OLS estimation of Equation (1.8) are shown in Table 1.22. At a significance level of 1%, all explanatory variables are significant. The value of 0.18 of the regression coefficient before **EUFAR** suggests that one unit of **EUFAR** change, with other variables held constant, will lead to a 0.18% change in the long-term unemployment rate **LTUR** (and the natural rate of unemployment **NRU**) in the same direction. The positive sign of the regression coefficient before **EUFAR** contradicts theoretical expectations and could be explained by an increase in structural unemployment in Bulgaria as a result of innovations funded by European funds. The value of the regression coefficient before **GDPGR** (-0.35) means that one percentage change in the rate of quarterly real GDP growth, with other variables held constant, will cause a change of 0.35% in the rate of long-term unemployment and the natural rate of unemployment in the opposite direction. The negative sign of the coefficient before **GDPGR** is in line with the theoretical expectations of a negative link between economic growth and the unemployment rate.

Table 1.22. Estimates of the parameters of Equation (1.8) for the period 2010-2015

Parameter	Estimate	Standard error	t-statistic	Probability
Intercept	6.45	0.27	23.66	0.00
EUFAR	0.18	0.06	3.08	0.00
GDPGR	-0.35	0.07	-5.03	0.00

Source: Prepared by the author

The value of the coefficient of determination (0.63) shows that 63% of the changes in the long-term unemployment rate in Bulgaria can be explained by changes in the rate of absorption of the EU funds and in real GDP growth rate. The probability of the F-statistic (0.00) indicates that the alternative hypothesis of the adequacy of the regression model is accepted. The acceptance of the alternative hypothesis does not mean that the model specification is the best possible but only that the regression model adequately reflects the relationship between dependent variable and independent variables.

The serial correlation LM test (see Table 1.23) confirmed the zero hypothesis of the absence of a serial correlation of residuals.

Table 1.23. Serial correlation LM test on the residuals of Equation (1.8)

Breusch-Godfrey Serial Correlation LM Test:				
F-statistic	1.537751	Prob. F(2,19)		0.2404
Obs*R-squared	3.343619	Prob. Chi-Square(2)		0.1879
Test Equation:				
Dependent Variable: RESID				
Method: Least Squares				
Date: 05/21/17 Time: 15:04				
Sample: 2010Q1 2015Q4				
Included observations: 24				
Presample missing value lagged residuals set to zero.				
Variable	Coefficient	Std. Error	t-Statistic	Prob.
C	0.226875	0.296586	0.764955	0.4537
EUFAR	-0.071497	0.071019	-1.006723	0.3267
GDPGR	-0.004687	0.067286	-0.069653	0.9452
RESID(-1)	0.442459	0.275271	1.607359	0.1245
RESID(-2)	0.069364	0.231619	0.299476	0.7678
R-squared	0.139317	Mean dependent var		-5.09E-16
Adjusted R-squared	-0.041879	S.D. dependent var		0.630816
S.E. of regression	0.643890	Akaike info criterion		2.140474
Sum squared resid	7.877288	Schwarz criterion		2.385901
Log likelihood	-20.68568	Hannan-Quinn criter.		2.205586
F-statistic	0.768876	Durbin-Watson stat		1.790266
Prob(F-statistic)	0.558668			

Source: Prepared by the author

The residual heteroscedasticity test (see Table 1.24) confirmed the null hypothesis of the absence of heteroscedasticity in Equation (1.8).

Table 1.24. Heteroscedasticity test (ARCH) on the residuals of Equation (1.8)

Heteroscedasticity Test: ARCH				
F-statistic	1.306806	Prob. F(1,21)		0.2658
Obs*R-squared	1.347415	Prob. Chi-Square(1)		0.2457
Test Equation:				
Dependent Variable: RESID^2				
Method: Least Squares				
Date: 05/21/17 Time: 15:11				
Sample (adjusted): 2010Q2 2015Q4				
Included observations: 23 after adjustments				
Variable	Coefficient	Std. Error	t-Statistic	Prob.
C	0.476185	0.111953	4.253430	0.0004
RESID^2(-1)	-0.242461	0.212098	-1.143156	0.2658
R-squared	0.058583	Mean dependent var		0.382627
Adjusted R-squared	0.013754	S.D. dependent var		0.368896
S.E. of regression	0.366350	Akaike info criterion		0.912488
Sum squared resid	2.818465	Schwarz criterion		1.011227
Log likelihood	-8.493614	Hannan-Quinn criter.		0.937321
F-statistic	1.306806	Durbin-Watson stat		2.163249
Prob(F-statistic)	0.265839			

Source: Prepared by the author

The requirement of normal residual distribution is observed in Equation (1.8) (see Figure 1.4). The probability of the Jarque-Bera statistic is 0.44, which gives reason to accept the zero hypothesis of a normal residual distribution.

Figure 1.4. Histogram of the residuals of Equation (1.8)

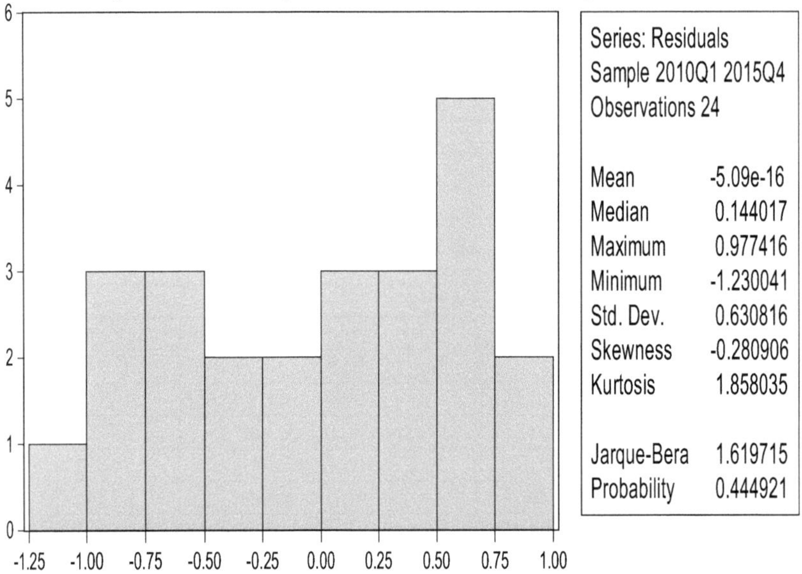

Source: Prepared by the author

The Ramsey's RESET Test confirmed the zero hypothesis of the lack of errors in the specification of Equation (1.8) at the 5% significance level (see Table 1.25).

Table 1.25. Regression Specification Error Test on Equation (1.8)

Ramsey RESET Test				
Equation: EQ_LTUR				
Specification: LTUR C EUFAR GDPGR				
Omitted Variables: Squares of fitted values				
	Value	df	Probability	
t-statistic	1.965286	20	0.0634	
F-statistic	3.862349	(1, 20)	0.0634	
Likelihood ratio	4.237670	1	0.0395	
F-test summary:				
	Sum of Sq.	df	Mean Squares	
Test SSR	1.481399	1	1.481399	
Restricted SSR	9.152373	21	0.435827	
Unrestricted SSR	7.670974	20	0.383549	
Unrestricted SSR	7.670974	20	0.383549	
LR test summary:				
	Value	df		
Restricted LogL	-22.48604	21		
Unrestricted LogL	-20.36720	20		
Unrestricted Test Equation:				
Dependent Variable: LTUR				
Method: Least Squares				
Date: 05/21/17 Time: 15:17				
Sample: 2010Q1 2015Q4				
Included observations: 24				
Variable	Coefficient	Std. Error	t-Statistic	Prob.
C	20.22724	7.015501	2.883221	0.0092
EUFAR	0.925520	0.382615	2.418930	0.0252
GDPGR	-1.737378	0.711365	-2.442314	0.0240
FITTED^2	-0.327604	0.166695	-1.965286	0.0634
R-squared	0.687302	Mean dependent var		6.331879
Adjusted R-squared	0.640397	S.D. dependent var		1.032758
S.E. of regression	0.619313	Akaike info criterion		2.030600
Sum squared resid	7.670974	Schwarz criterion		2.226942
Log likelihood	-20.36720	Hannan-Quinn criter.		2.082690
F-statistic	14.65313	Durbin-Watson stat		1.568356
Prob(F-statistic)	0.000028			

Source: Prepared by the author

Empirical estimation of the impact of the absorbed EU funds on the potential GDP of Bulgaria

Assumptions and methodology

The methodology of Todorov (2017) with the following modifications was used to assess the impact of the absorbed EU funds on the potential GDP of Bulgaria:

- The capacity utilization in industry was removed from the formula for calculating the potential output;
- The effect of EU funds on capital stocks was accounted for - the absorbed EU funds were transformed from nominal to real terms by deflation with a price index (deflator) and were added to the amount of capital stock;
- The impact of the absorbed EU funds on the long-term unemployment rate was accounted for - the change in the rate of absorption of the EU funds by 1% leads to 0.18% change in the long-term unemployment rate in the same direction (see Section 3);
- The effect of the absorbed EU funds on total factor productivity (TFP) was accounted for. TFP was calculated as a residual after taking into account the effects of the absorbed EU funds on employment and on capital stocks.

Alike Gladnishki (2005) and Todorov (2017), in the present study the potential GDP of Bulgaria was estimated through an approach based on a two-factor production function of Cobb Douglas:

$$\textbf{(1.9) } \mathbf{YPOT = A * K^{\alpha} * LPOT^{\beta}}$$

where **YPOT** is Bulgaria's potential output, **A** is total factor productivity, **K** is capital stock, **α** is the elasticity of output with respect to capital, **LPOT** is the potential (optimal) employment of labor resources and **β** is the elasticity of output with respect to labor.

The elasticity coefficients were estimated via an equilibrium approach, which is based on the income structure of Bulgaria's GDP and was used by Raleva (2013) and Todorov (2015). According to this approach the whole mixed income is treated as a labor income. The labor income is calculated by adding to the compensation of employees **CE** one third of the sum of the net mixed income **NMI** and the net operating surplus **NOS**. The capital income equals two thirds of the sum of the net mixed income **NMI** and the net operating surplus **NOS**. The coefficients **α** and **β** are calculated as

$$(1.10)\ \alpha = \frac{2}{3}(NOS + NMI)/(CE + NOS + NMI)$$

$$(1.11)\ \beta = [CE + 1/3\ (NOS + NMI)]\ /\ (CE + NOS + NMI)$$

The sum of **α** and **β** is 1. The average values of **α** and **β** for the period 1997-2015 are respectively 0.35 and 0.65 and were used in estimating Bulgaria's potential output.

Since the Bulgarian national statistics does not provide data on capital stock, one of the methodological problems, related to potential output estimation, is how to calculate the size of capital stock. Two approaches can be used to solve this problem – the perpetual inventory method (Ganev, 2005) and the constant capital-output ratio approach (Minassian, 2008; Raleva, 2013; Todorov and Durova, 2016). In this paper the constant capital-output ratio approach is employed.

The capital-output ratio **K/Y** is considered constant in economic theory. In empirical studies this ratio varies between 2 and 3. For Bulgaria the used values of the capital-output ratio are 2.5 (Minassian, 2008), 2.3 (Raleva, 2013) and 2.2 (Todorov, 2016). For the purpose of this study the used value of the capital-output ratio is 2.2. It is calculated as the average gross-capital-formation-to-change-in-real-GDP ratio for the period 1998-2008 (in accordance with the assumption of

Harrod and Domar that the average and the marginal productivity of capital are equal). Hence, the actual real size of capital stock **K** can be determined by multiplying the real GDP **Y** by the capital/output ratio **K/Y,** whose value is 2.2:

$$(1.12)\ K = Y * K/Y = Y * 2.2$$

The absorbed EU funds have the character of investments, so in the present analysis it is assumed that they directly increase the amount of capital stock in the Bulgarian economy. Since the absorbed EU funds are in nominal terms, they should be deflated and transformed in real terms before being added to capital stock. The increase in capital stock ΔK_t in year **t** as a result of the absorption of EU funds EUF_t in the same year **t** can be calculated using the formula

$$(1.13)\ \Delta K_t = EUF_t / PI_t$$

where: ΔK_t – increase in capital stock in year **t**; EUF_t – absorbed EU funds in year **t**; PI_t – price index (deflator).

For the estimation of capital stock and the impact of the absorbed EU funds on it were used annual data of Eurostat (on Bulgaria's GDP and deflator at prices of 2010) and KPMG (on the amount of the absorbed EU funds in Bulgaria) for the period 2010-2015.

Table 1.26. Capital stock and absorbed EU funds, millions of Euros at prices of 2010

Year	Capital stock with the absorbed EU funds	Absorbed EU funds	Capital stock without the absorbed EU fund
2010	84 107	469	83 638
2011	85 718	568	85 149
2012	85 744	933	84 811
2013	86 484	1 254	85 230
2014	87 633	1 435	86 197
2015	90 803	1 099	89 704
Total		5 760	

Source: Prepared by the author

The effect of the absorbed EU funds on capital stock in the Bulgarian economy is shown in Table 1.26. For the period 2010-2015, the absorbed EU funds increased capital stock in Bulgaria by nearly 5.8 billion euro at 2010 prices. It can be concluded that the funds of the European Union are an important source of investment financing and of expanding the production capacity of the Bulgarian economy.

Two indicators can be used to measure labor input in the production function - the number of employees or the number of hours worked in an economy. In the present study, as in Minassian (2008), Ganev (2005) and Todorov (2015, 2016 and 2017), the first indicator was chosen.

Potential (optimal) employment of labor resources is calculated by the formula

$$(1.14)\ LPOT = LF * (1 - LTUR - OREULC + IREULC)$$

Where: **LPOT** – potential (optimal) employment of labor resources; **LF** – labor force; **LTUR** – rate of long-term unemployment; **OREULC** - outflow rate of employees under labor contract; **IREULC** - inflow rate of employees under labor contract.

Potential employment and the effect of the absorbed EU funds on it are shown in Table 1.27. It was accounted for that a change in the rate of absorption of EU funds by 1% leads to 0.18% change in the rate of long-term unemployment in the same direction. An increase in absorbed EU funds ceteris paribus causes a reduction in potential employment, as a possible reason for this is an increase in structural unemployment due to financing of innovations with European funds.

Table 1.27. Impact of EU funds on potential employment

Year	Potential employment in the presence of EU funds, thousands of persons	EU funds absorption rate, percentage	Potential employment in the lack of EU funds, thousands of persons
2010	3 247	7	3 290
2011	3 164	9	3 218
2012	3 143	15	3 234
2013	3 165	20	3 287
2014	3 189	23	3 329
2015	3 203	18	3 312

Source: Prepared by the author

For each year of the 2010-2015 period, total factor productivity was calculated using the formula

$$\textbf{(1.15)}\ A_t = Y_t / (K_t^{0.35} * L_t^{0.65})$$

Where: A_t – total factor productivity in year **t**; Y_t – GDP in year **t** at 2010 prices in millions of euro; K_t – capital stock in year **t** at 2010 prices in millions of euro; L_t – number of employed persons in year **t** (in thousands).

The values of total factor productivity in the presence and in the absence of EU funds are shown in Table 1.28. It was accounted for that capital stock and employment are different in the presence and in the absence of EU funds of EU funds. Total factor productivity is higher in the presence of EU funds than in their absence. Possible explanations for the positive effect of the absorbed EU funds on total factor productivity are improvements in the technology and the infrastructure of the Bulgarian economy as a result of the realization of EU funded projects. As an increase in the absorption rate of EU funds leads to an increase in the long-term unemployment rate (see Section 3), it is unlikely that the increase in total factor productivity is due to a rise in the quantity and quality of human capital. If the quantity and quality of human capital rose, the increase in the absorption of EU funds would cause a decline in the rate of long-term unemployment.

Table 1.28.: Total factor productivity with and without EU funds

Year	Total factor productivity with EU funds	Total factor productivity without EU funds
2010	3,90	3,88
2011	4,05	4,01
2012	4,08	4,01
2013	4,10	4,01
2014	4,09	3,99
2015	4,14	4,07

Source: Prepared by the author

The values of the potential GDP of Bulgaria in the presence and in the absence of EU funds are shown in Table 1.29. In each year of the analyzed period 2010-2015 the potential GDP in the presence of utilized EU funds was higher than the potential GDP in the absence of EU funds. For the entire period 2010-2015 the absorbed EU funds increased Bulgaria's potential GDP by EUR 311 million at 2010 prices. The positive effects of the EU funds on potential GDP (generated by the increase in capital stock and total factor productivity) are greater than their negative effects on potential output (caused by the decrease in potential employment as a result of the increase in the absorbed EU funds).

Table 1.29. Potential GDP with and without EU funds, million Euros at prices of 2010

Year	Potential GDP with EU funds	Potential GDP without EU funds	Difference
2010	39 603	39 584	19
2011	40 638	40 608	30
2012	40 756	40 703	53
2013	41 287	41 209	78
2014	41 613	41 534	79
2015	42 773	42 721	52
Total		311	

Source: Prepared by the author

https://doi.org/10.2478/9783110619218-003

CHAPTER TWO. BULGARIA'S ECONOMIC GROWTH

2.1. Theoretical background

Economic growth can be defined as an increase in real output (gross income) or in real output (gross income) per capita. Growth reduces the burden of scarcity and can be used to solve national and international socio-economic problems.

Supply factors influencing growth are:

1. The quantity and quality of natural resources of a nation;
2. The quantity and quality of its human resources;
3. Its capital stock;
4. Technology.

There are two factors that are essential to whether the economy will realize its potential for growth - a sufficient level of aggregate demand and efficiency of resource allocation.

The principle of diminishing returns limits growth opportunities when one or more inputs have a fixed amount. This principle states that at a certain technological level adding additional units of one production factor (labor) to fixed amounts of other factors (land and capital) will eventually lead to reduced gross product per employee or in other words, to reducing productivity. Thomas Malthus used the law of diminishing returns to explain the widespread poverty that existed in his time. Specifically, he argued that rapid population growth combined with declining returns on agricultural production will keep real income per capita close to the level of survival (subsistence minimum).

Technological advances, growth of capital stock and improving the quality of labor and management increase productivity and neutralize the law of diminishing returns. Reducing the growth of labor productivity may cause a slowdown in the pace of growth in living standards and lead to inflation.

Growth of productive potential can be achieved only if aggregate demand is growing with an appropriate pace. Models of growth emphasize the possibilities of net investments to increase production capacity and show that the growth rate of the economy at full employment can be calculated as the quotient between the average propensity to save and the capital-output ratio. The average propensity to save and the pace of economic growth are positively related, and the relationship between the capital-output ratio and the growth rate is negative. The realization of the growth potential of the economy requires an adequate efficient allocation of resources.

Computer models of the Club of Rome forecasted a collapse of economic growth as a result of the discrepancy between the growth rates of population and production, and restrictions placed on this increase by scarce natural resources and environmental pollution. Members of the Club of Rome recommended policies of zero growth of the economy and population in order to avoid a sharp decline in living standards in the long term.

Criticism against models of the Club of Rome is in the following directions:

- Models of the Club of Rome are based on unrealistic assumptions;
- Models of the Club of Rome failed to adequately consider the effect of technological progress, which helps to overcome the scarcity of resources;
- Models of the Club of Rome overlook the role of mechanisms such as price system and changes in human behavior.

Economic growth is the main source to improve the standard of living over time. In the long term, even small differences in growth rates can have a huge effect on the standard of living in different countries. Growth accounting is a method of separating the growth of output into parts resulting from the growth of capital stock, growth of labor resources and productivity growth. These three factors contribute to long-term economic growth in each country.

The Solow model explores the relationship between growth, saving and capital accumulation over time. It predicts that in the absence of productivity growth the economy will reach a steady state in which the aggregate production, consumption and capital per worker are constants. According to the Solow model, each of these conditions leads to higher output, consumption and capital per worker in the long term: an increase in the savings rate, a decline in the rate of population growth and a rise in productivity.

Endogenous growth theory attempts to explain but not take for granted productivity growth in the economy. One element of this approach emphasizes the formation of human capital, including the acquisition of skills and qualifications of workers. A second element focuses on research and development. Endogenous growth theorists argue that as the growth of capital and output causes an increase in human capital and innovation, the marginal productivity of capital for the economy as a whole may not be reduced. Implication of this theory is that the saving rate can influence the long-term rate of economic growth.

Government policies to improve the long-term standard of living include increasing the rate of saving and productivity. Possible ways to improve productivity are investing in public capital (infrastructure), stimulating the creation of human capital and the expansion of research and development.

2.2. Review of empirical research on Bulgaria's economic growth under the transition to a market-oriented economy

The economic growth of Bulgaria in the process of transition to a market economy was empirically investigated by Ganev (2005), Minassian (2008), Pirimova (2001 and 2014), Raleva (2013), Statev (2009), Todorov (2015) etc.

Ganev (2005), Minassian (2008) and Raleva (2013) applied the methodology "growth accounting" based on a two-factor Cobb-Douglas production function. Besides the common features in the methodology of these studies there are certain differences:

- The growth of capital stock in Ganev (2005) was estimated by the perpetual inventory method, while in Minassian (2008) and in Raleva (2013) – by the method of the constant ratio "capital stock/GDP";
- Minassian (2008) used the value of the ratio of "capital stock / GDP" 2.5 and Raleva (2013) - 2.3;
- For the measurement of employment Minassian (2008) and Ganev (2005) used the number of employees and Raleva (2013) - the number of hours worked in the economy;
- In assessing the elasticity coefficients, Minassian (2008) used the expenditure structure of GDP and Ganev (2005) and Raleva (2013) – the income structure of GDP.
- Ganev (2005), Minassian (2008), Raleva (2013) and Todorov (2015) reached similar conclusions:
- Total factor productivity and changes in capital stock are the main determinants of economic growth in Bulgaria on the supply side;
- Changes in employment have a little negative effect on growth, which is offset by the impact of total factor productivity and changes in capital stock.

Pirimova (2001) applied the early classical models of Smith, Ricardo, Wicksell and Feldman, as well as a base Keynesian model for analyzing the economic growth in Bulgaria in the process of transition to a market economy. This study confirmed the conclusion of a non-equilibrium nature of growth in Bulgaria in the transition to a market economy. This implies that efforts of macroeconomic management should be aimed not at achieving a balanced proportional growth but at reducing the large variations in growth rates over the years.

Pirimova (2014) focused more on the analysis of the economic cycle and its characteristics than on economic growth. Unlike other studies that adopt the assumption of a closed economy, Pirimova (2014) placed an emphasis on the openness of the Bulgarian economy and its dependence on global and regional trends. The results of the study of Pirimova (2014) showed that for a relatively smooth economic dynamics are needed measures to affect both the real and the financial sector, actions to stimulate long-term economic growth and common strategies for economic development of the EU.

Statev (2009) emphasized the role of the financial sector to economic growth in Bulgaria. This study is important because a key problem of the Bulgarian economy is the transformation of savings into investments. Statev employed complex methodology and reaches recommendations on improving the efficiency of the financial sector in the country and on increasing its positive impact on growth.

Todorov (2015) combined an econometric approach (least squares) and an equilibrium approach (growth accounting) to assess the elasticities in the production function and to identify the contributions of the main factors on the supply side to economic growth in Bulgaria under the CBA. Like Minassian (2008) and Raleva (2013), Todorov (2015) employed the method of the constant ratio "capital stock/GDP" for the calculation of the growth of capital stock. In the study of Todorov (2015) employment was measured by the number of the employed persons in the economy, like in Minassian (2008) and Ganev (2005).

2.3. Bulgaria's short-term and long-term economic growth under a currency board arrangement

The dynamics of output can be analyzed in two time dimensions – short run and long run. The short-term dynamics is calculated at a chain (floating) base, i.e. in comparison with the previous year. The long-term dynamics is calculated at a constant base; the base year is usually the first year of the period. The short-term developments in real GDP of Bulgaria are shown in Table 1, and the long-term - in Table 2.1.

Table 2.1. Growth of real GDP compared to the previous year

Year	GGD growth rate
1997	-1,09%
1998	3,46%
1999	-5,65%
2000	6,04%
2001	3,80%
2002	4,48%
2003	5,36%
2004	6,56%
2005	5,96%
2006	6,47%
2007	6,91%
2008	5,75%
2009	-5,01%
2010	0,66%
2011	1,98%
2012	0,49%
2013	1,07%

Source: Website of the National Statistical Institute of Bulgaria http://www.nsi.bg/

Short-term rates of growth of real output in Bulgaria in the period 1997-2013 were characterized by a pronounced unevenness and alternating negative and positive rates. This period can be divided into three sub-periods depending on the stability and the magnitude of the growth rates of real GDP.

The first sub-period of 1996-1999 was dominated by negative rates of change in real GDP. This sub-period was characterized by instability and frequent changes in the direction and the growth rate of output. In the second sub-period 2000-2008 were registered stable and high growth rates of output. The third sub-period 2009-2013, began with a collapse of real GDP in 2009, followed by years of slow and painful recovery. The decline in output in 2009 was caused by the global financial and economic crisis, which had an adverse shock impact on the Bulgarian economy. The large decline in real GDP was indicative of the strength of the impact of this exogenous factor, which in a sense even determined the behavior of domestic production. It also showed that the effects of the global crisis spread in time, as the dynamics of domestic production depended on its restriction or deepening. So the next positive rates after 2010 should not be interpreted rashly as a sign of a lasting reversal of the direction of change in real GDP.

Table 2.2. Growth of real GDP compared to 1996

Year	GGD growth rate
1997	-1,09%
1998	2,34%
1999	-3,44%
2000	2,39%
2001	6,28%
2002	11,04%
2003	16,99%
2004	24,66%
2005	32,09%
2006	40,63%
2007	50,35%
2008	59,00%
2009	51,03%
2010	52,02%
2011	55,03%
2012	55,80%
2013	57,46%

Source: Website of the National Statistical Institute of Bulgaria http://www.nsi.bg/

The long-term dynamics of real GDP (at a constant base 1996) for the period was generally upward. The maximum level of aggregate production was reached in 2008 - an increase of 59% compared to 1996. This increase was a result of the stable and high growth rates in the years before the global crisis. After the collapse of nearly 8% in 2009 compared to 2008 at a base of 1996, the pace of GDP growth remained low but stable until 2013. Of the size of the 2009 collapse is indicative the fact that by the end of 2013 the real GDP of Bulgaria still failed to reach its highest pre-crisis level of 2008.

2.4. The dynamics of aggregate demand's components as a determinant of the short-term economic growth

Table 2.3. Final expenditure structure of Bulgaria's real GDP in million levs at prices of 2010

Year	Private consumption expenditure	Gross investment	Government spending	Net exports	GDP
1996	29114	2473	7964	13419	47299
1997	24034	4188	7295	15639	46784
1998	24470	5396	8577	10393	48404
1999	26733	6379	8911	2961	45671
2000	28721	7401	9624	1024	48429
2001	30825	8883	9901	-915	50268
2002	31971	9602	10054	-499	52521
2003	34020	10835	10966	-2320	55334
2004	36804	12324	11456	-3299	58964
2005	38868	15622	11612	-5173	62475
2006	42217	17654	12050	-8393	66518
2007	46973	19969	12209	-11226	71112
2008	48691	24358	12081	-12665	75205
2009	45584	20116	11152	-6188	71436
2010	45826	16431	11389	-2009	71904
2011	46650	15674	11589	-1005	73329
2012	48464	15980	11471	-2696	73690
2013	47371	15968	11793	-920	74475
2014	48320	16412	12244	-1715	75745

Source: Website of the National Statistical Institute of Bulgaria http://www.nsi.bg/

The expenditure structure of GDP shows the elements of aggregate expenditure (aggregate demand). Its dynamics is important primarily for short-term rates of economic growth.

In absolute terms, each component of aggregate demand for the period 1996-2014 had its own specific dynamics (see Table 2.3). The patterns of change in consumer spending of private sector and in gross investment resembled that of GDP, indicating that consumer spending of private sector and gross investment were the main determinants of growth on the demand side for the period 1996-2014 as a whole. Government expenditure was relatively stable. The most unstable component of aggregate expenditure were net exports, which were negative in periods of boom and positive in periods of crisis.

Table 2.4. Growth rates of the components of the final expenditure structure of real GDP compared to the previous year

Year	Private consumption expenditure	Gross investment	Government spending	Net exports	GDP
1997	-17,45	69,36	-8,41	16,54	-1,09
1998	1,82	28,83	17,58	-33,54	3,46
1999	9,25	18,23	3,89	-71,51	-5,65
2000	7,44	16,02	8,00	-65,41	6,04
2001	7,33	20,02	2,88	-189,35	3,80
2002	3,72	8,10	1,54	-45,45	4,48
2003	6,41	12,84	9,07	364,62	5,36
2004	8,18	13,74	4,47	42,24	6,56
2005	5,61	26,77	1,36	56,80	5,96
2006	8,62	13,01	3,77	62,23	6,47
2007	11,27	13,11	1,32	33,77	6,91
2008	3,66	21,98	-1,05	12,81	5,75
2009	-6,38	-17,41	-7,69	-51,14	-5,01
2010	0,53	-18,32	2,13	-67,54	0,66
2011	1,80	-4,61	1,75	-49,95	1,98
2012	3,89	1,96	-1,02	168,12	0,49
2013	-2,26	-0,08	2,81	-65,88	1,07
2014	2,00	2,78	3,82	86,48	1,71

Source: Website of the National Statistical Institute of Bulgaria http://www.nsi.bg/

The dynamics of rates of change of expenditure components of GDP (see Table 2.4) shows that the main determinant of economic growth on the demand side in times of crisis were net exports and during an upswing - consumption and investment. In 2010-2014, the weak economic growth in Bulgaria was mainly due to positive net exports. The main reason for the increase in exports in recent years were the exports of products with low added value (mainly raw materials). Bulgaria cannot count on such a model of export-oriented growth, as it would not survive in the medium and in the long term because of the limited resources of the Bulgarian economy.

Table 2.5. Final expenditure structure of real GDP (a percentage of real GDP)

Year	Private consumption expenditure	Gross investment	Government spending	Net exports
1996	61,55	5,23	16,84	28,37
1997	51,37	8,95	15,59	33,43
1998	50,55	11,15	17,72	21,47
1999	58,53	13,97	19,51	6,48
2000	59,31	15,28	19,87	2,11
2001	61,32	17,67	19,70	-1,82
2002	60,87	18,28	19,14	-0,95
2003	61,48	19,58	19,82	-4,19
2004	62,42	20,90	19,43	-5,60
2005	62,21	25,01	18,59	-8,28
2006	63,47	26,54	18,12	-12,62
2007	66,05	28,08	17,17	-15,79
2008	64,74	32,39	16,06	-16,84
2009	63,81	28,16	15,61	-8,66
2010	63,73	22,85	15,84	-2,79
2011	63,62	21,37	15,80	-1,37
2012	65,77	21,69	15,57	-3,66
2013	63,61	21,44	15,84	-1,24
2014	63,79	21,67	16,17	-2,26
Average	61,49	20,01	17,49	0,31
Standard deviation	4,19	6,90	1,69	13,64

Source: Website of the National Statistical Institute of Bulgaria http://www.nsi.bg/

For the period 1996-2014, the largest component of the expenditure structure of GDP was the consumer spending of the private sector. Its average value for the period was 61% of GDP, and its standard deviation was 4% of GDP. These values correspond to the values of developed economies.

The average share of government spending in GDP was 17% and its standard deviation was 2%. Government spending was the most stable component of the expenditure structure of GDP. The government adheres to a policy of sustainable share of government spending in GDP and does not use discretionary and counter-cyclical fiscal policy as a tool of macroeconomic management.

Gross investment played a crucial role in the growth of real GDP in 1998, 2005 and 2008, as the effect of higher investment exceeded the impact of negative foreign trade balance. The average value of gross investment for the period was 20% of GDP, and its standard deviation was 7%.

The positive values of net exports during the period 1996-2000 were offset by their further negative values by 2014. The average value of net exports for the period 1996-2013 was 0, which is in line with theoretical postulates that the long-period net exports tend to 0. The standard deviation of net exports was 13% of GDP, making it the most volatile component of the expenditure structure of GDP during the analyzed period.

2.5. The dynamics of the factors of the long-run economic growth in Bulgaria

The saving rate

The savings rate is a determinant of long-term economic growth. Its increase means a sacrifice in terms of a lower current consumption for the purpose of a higher future consumption. It is considered in economic theory that the rising of the share of saving in GDP is positively related to the long-term growth rate of GDP and the standards of living. The explanation is that the higher saving means higher investment in physical capital, human capital, infrastructure and research and development, which increase the production capacity and the productivity of the national economy.

The savings rate **s** is the share of national saving **S** in **GDP**:

(2.1) s = S / GDP

Under the equilibrium condition of the goods market in an open economy, national saving **S** is the sum of gross investment (gross fixed capital formation) **GCF** and the current account balance **CAB:**

(2.2) S = GCF + CAB

The saving rate **SR** can be calculated as

(2.3) s = (GCF + CAB) / GDP

Table 1.6. Saving rate (the percentage share of the sum of gross fixed capital formation and the current account balance in GDP)

Year	Saving rate
1997	13,74%
1998	18,27%
1999	14,71%
2000	13,90%
2001	15,98%
2002	18,25%
2003	16,95%
2004	17,25%
2005	16,49%
2006	15,16%
2007	9,65%
2008	14,91%
2009	20,26%
2010	21,45%
2011	21,73%
2012	21,27%
2013	23,18%

Source: Eurostat

In the movement of the saving rate in Bulgaria under a currency board (see Table 1.6) can clearly be distinguished two periods. In the first period (1997-2007) the dynamics of the saving rate was chaotic and often altered the direction of its variation. The prevailing in the first period decreasing trends found expression in the decline in the saving rate from 13.74% in 1997 to 9.65% in 2007. The main reason for the reduction in the saving rate during the period 1997-2007 were the large (about a quarter of GDP) current account deficits, which were not compensated even by strong investment activity in the years before the global financial crisis. In the second period (2007-2013) the saving rate marked a steady upward trend, increasing from 9.65% in 2007 to 23.18% in 2013. The increase in the saving rate during the second period was due to the decline of the deficit of the current account balance, which in certain years even turned into a surplus (in 2011 and 2013). It can be concluded that in Bulgaria as a small open economy a major determinant of the rate of saving is the current account balance. Despite its upward dynamics in 2007-2013, as a whole the saving rate under the CBA is unstable and below the EU average.

The rate of productivity growth

Total factor productivity is the most important determinant of the long-term economic growth and the standard of living of a nation. Under the conditions of limited quantities of factors of production, the permanent improvement of production efficiency is the only way to continuously improve the welfare of a nation. Modern endogenous growth models refute predictions of earlier models that a certain amount of the population will lead to diminishing marginal productivity of factors of production and inability to raise the living standards of people. Endogenous models prove that it is possible that the marginal productivity of factors of production is not decreasing but constant or even increasing due to the increased productivity caused by the formation of human capital, research and development and investment in public infrastructure.

The dynamics of total factor productivity in Bulgaria is analyzed in section 2.6. Supply-side factors of economic growth.

The rate of population growth

According to economic theory, the rate of population growth is negatively related to the rate of the long-term economic growth and the long-term standard of living of the nation. As a measure of the living standards traditionally is used the real GDP per capita, which is the ratio between real GDP and the number of population. When real GDP grows at a higher rate than the number of population, the living standard of the nation increases. Conversely, if real GDP grows at a slower pace than the number of population, then the standard of living of the nation falls.

Table 2.7. Average annual number of population in Bulgaria

Year	Average annual number of population
2000	8170172
2001	7913301
2002	7868900
2003	7823557
2004	7781161
2005	7739900
2006	7699020
2007	7659764
2008	7623395
2009	7585131
2010	7534289
2011	7348328
2012	7305888
2013	7265115

Source: Website of the National Statistical Institute of Bulgaria http://www.nsi.bg/

The average population in Bulgaria in the period 2000-2013 steadily declined as a result of the negative natural and mechanical growth (see Table 2.7). This reduction had two opposite effects on GDP per capita - quantitative and qualitative. On the one hand, the decline of the population increased the GDP per capita and raised the standard of living of the nation. On the other hand, the qualitative effects of the reduction of the population are expressed in productivity losses because the population decline is due to the deterioration of the population age structure (aging) and the migration of young and able-bodied Bulgarians abroad, where Bulgaria ranks first in the European Union (Naidenova and Mihova, 2010).

Table 2.8. Percentage change in the average annual number of population in Bulgaria

Year	Population growth rate
2001	-3,14%
2002	-0,56%
2003	-0,58%
2004	-0,54%
2005	-0,53%
2006	-0,53%
2007	-0,51%
2008	-0,47%
2009	-0,50%
2010	-0,67%
2011	-2,47%
2012	-0,58%
2013	-0,56%

Source: Website of the National Statistical Institute of Bulgaria http://www.nsi.bg/

The percentage change in the average annual number of population in Bulgaria was permanently negative in the period 2001-2013 because of the negative natural and mechanical growth.

Employment

Two indicators can be used to measure employment - the number of employees or the number of hours worked in the economy. Table 2.9 shows the dynamics of employment, as measured by the number of hours worked in Bulgaria.

Table 2.9. Number of hours worked in Bulgaria, in thousands

Year	Number of hours worked
1995	6019126
1996	6175118
1997	5980710
1998	5722002
1999	5539651
2000	5313110
2001	5310297
2002	5320556
2003	5442215
2004	5662198
2005	5797417
2006	5974685
2007	6165971
2008	6460476
2009	6172380
2010	5927815
2011	5792925
2012*	5650971
2013*	5628429

Source: Website of the National Statistical Institute of Bulgaria http://www.nsi.bg/

The dynamics of the number of hours worked in Bulgaria indicates the ascending and the descending trends in the Bulgarian economy during the transition to a market-oriented economy. In the period 1995-2001 there was a decline in employment, as measured by the number of hours worked. This decline reflects the crisis transformation processes of the transition. In 2002-2008, labor market trends overturned, as employment increased. Employment growth in the period

2002-2008 was due to the high and sustainable economic growth caused by the change in the expectations of economic agents as a result of the accession of Bulgaria to the EU and the massive inflows of foreign capital in the country. After 2008 there was a reduction in employment.

Table 2.10. Percentage growth rate of the hours worked in Bulgaria compared to the previous year

Year	Growth rate of employment ΔL/L
1996	2,59%
1997	-3,15%
1998	-4,33%
1999	-3,19%
2000	-4,09%
2001	-0,05%
2002	0,19%
2003	2,29%
2004	4,04%
2005	2,39%
2006	3,06%
2007	3,20%
2008	4,78%
2009	-4,46%
2010	-3,96%
2011	-2,28%
2012*	-2,45%
2013*	-0,40%

Source: Website of the National Statistical Institute of Bulgaria http://www.nsi.bg/

In the crisis years 1996 and 1997 the lowest values of real GDP were accompanied by employment levels, which were higher than the average for the entire period. The growth rates of employment remained negative until 2000 as a results of the occurring changes in the economy and the shift to a currency board arrangement (see Table 2.10). After 2000, the employment growth rate was positive and particularly high in 2004. The positive developments in employment in the period

2002-2008 were due to the stable and high growth rates of real GDP. The positive impact of output on employment occurred with a lag of two years. The negative influence of the dynamics of real GDP on the labor market, however, appeared immediately - employment dropped immediately when low positive or negative rates of change of output were recorded (see 2009). The positive growth rates of real GDP in the period 2010-2013 were too low to cause an overturn in the negative trends in the labor market. For such an overturn to happen, as experience showed, are needed at least two years of a high and sustainable economic growth.

Investment

Investment is a key determinant of economic growth both on the supply side and the demand side of the economy. On the demand side the growth of investment expenditure increases aggregate expenditure through the mechanism of the multiplier. In turn, the GDP change also affects investment through the principle of the accelerator. On the supply side investments directly increase the productive capacity of the economy (physical capital) and indirectly can contribute to productivity growth by building infrastructure, formation of human capital and research and development.

Table 2.11. Dynamics of the percentage share of gross investment in GDP

Year	Gross investment/GDP
1996	5%
1997	9%
1998	11%
1999	14%
2000	15%
2001	18%
2002	18%
2003	20%
2004	21%
2005	25%
2006	27%
2007	28%
2008	32%
2009	28%
2010	23%
2011	21%
2012	22%
2013	21%
2014*	22%

Source: Website of the National Statistical Institute of Bulgaria http://www.nsi.bg/

The dynamics of the share of gross investment in GDP (see Table 2.11) indicates that it is among the most volatile and contributing to the growth components of aggregate expenditure. The dynamics of the share of gross investment in GDP can be divided into three periods:

- 1996-2008 - during this period there was a steady upward dynamics of the share of gross investment in GDP. The reason for the increase in investment activity was the improvement of business environment in Bulgaria as a consequence of the introduction of the currency board arrangement, the accession to the EU, the entry of foreign banks on the Bulgarian market and others;

- 2009-2011 - in this period there was a decrease in gross investment arising from the global financial crisis and the debt crisis in the Eurozone;
- 2012-2014 - in this period gross investment remained relatively unchanged. Despite the positive trends in the European and the world economy, Bulgaria continued its slow and painful recovery from the crisis. This period of stagnation could be explained with both external and internal causes. The external causes are the debt crisis in Greece, the EU imposed sanctions against Russia, the conflict in Ukraine, the war in Syria and the continuing refugee flow from North Africa and the Middle East. The internal reasons are the frequent change of governments, the failure of Corporate Commercial Bank, the inconsistent and ineffective macroeconomic policies (expressed in the negative financial result of the Bulgarian National Bank and the decline in foreign exchange reserves of Bulgaria in 2013, as well as in the shaken confidence of economic agents in the macroeconomic management and the macroeconomic stability of the country).

Table 2.12. Dynamics of gross investment in million levs

Year	Gross investment
1996	2473
1997	4188
1998	5396
1999	6379
2000	7401
2001	8883
2002	9602
2003	10835
2004	12324
2005	15622
2006	17654
2007	19969
2008	24358
2009	20116
2010	16431
2011	15674
2012	15980
2013	15968
2014*	16412

Source: Website of the National Statistical Institute of Bulgaria http://www.nsi.bg/

In the dynamics of the absolute amount of gross investment for the period 1996-2014 (see Table 2.12) are distinctly outlined three sub-periods. The first sub-period (1996-2008 years) was characterized by a sustainable increase in gross investment, which resulted from various factors - the introduction of the currency board arrangement in 1997, the entry of foreign banks in the banking sector and Bulgaria's accession to the EU in 2007. All these factors contributed to the increased confidence of local and foreign investors and to the improvement of the investment climate in the country. The second sub-period (2009-2010) was marked by a sharp decline in investment activity due to the global financial and economic crisis. In the third sub-period (2010-2014) gross investment stabilized at a level of 15-16 billion levs per annum, which, however, is well below the maximum pre-crisis level of 2008 of 24 billion levs This trend of stagnation of gross investment is one of the main reasons for the slow and painful recovery of economic growth in the country from the collapse in 2009.

2.6. Supply-side factors of economic growth

The basic shortcoming of the Keynesian growth models - the use of short-term analytical tools, has been overcome by the neoclassical models. Therefore, the neoclassical models are regarded as the first real models of economic growth. The growth analysis in the neoclassical theory is based on the Cobb-Douglas production function. The Cobb-Douglas production function underlies the concept of growth accounting, which was initially proposed by Abramovitz (1956) and Solow (1957) and further developed by Denison (1967 and 1985), Maddison (1982) and others. The growth accounting approach attempts to assess the impact of the main supply-side determinants on economic growth.

The output growth rate can be represented as a sum of growth rates of technology improvement (the so called total factor productivity), capital stock and labor input (with the latter two being weighted by their shares in the gross income):

(2.4) $$\Delta Y / Y = \Delta A / A + \alpha^* \Delta K / K + \beta * L / L$$

where:

$\Delta Y/Y$ - rate of output growth;

$\Delta A/A$ - rate of productivity growth;

$\Delta K/K$ - rate of capital growth;

$\Delta L/L$ - rate of labor growth;

α - elasticity of output with respect to capital

β - elasticity of output with respect to labor.

In Formula (2.4) the elasticity of output with respect to capital **α** shows the percentage increase in output, caused by a one percent increase in capital stock and the elasticity of output with respect to labor **β** represents the percentage increase in output, caused by a one percent increase in the amount of labor input. Formula (2.4), referred to as growth accounting equation, is a production function modified to a growth rate form.

Formula (2.4) states that output growth **ΔY/Y** can be broken into three components:

1) Output growth, caused by productivity growth - **ΔA/A**;
2) Output growth, caused by increased capital stock - **α ΔK/K**;
3) Output growth, caused by increased labor inputs - **β ΔL/L**.

The growth accounting technique rests on the following three assumptions:

1. Constant returns to scale;
2. Diminishing marginal productivity of capital and labor;
3. Perfect competition in the economy.

Growth accounting provides an empirical measure of the relative importance of the three components of output growth. Usually growth accounting includes four stages of analysis as follows:

Stage 1: Calculate the growth rates of output, capital and labor in the whole economy for the analyzed time periods.

Stage 2: Estimate the values of the elasticities of output with respect to capital **(α)** and labor **(β)**.

Stage 3: Calculate the contribution of capital to economic growth as **α ΔK/K** and the contribution of labor to economic growth as **β ΔL/L**.

Stage 4: The part of economic growth that can be attributed neither to capital nor to labor growth is explained by a rise in the total factor productivity **A**. The rate of productivity change **ΔA/A** is calculated from the Formula:

$$\Delta A / A = \Delta Y / Y - \alpha^* \Delta K / K - \beta * L / L \qquad \textbf{(2.5)}$$

Formula (2.5) is a modification of the growth accounting equation (Formula 2.4), with **ΔA/A** written on the left side of the equation. In this way the growth accounting approach treats the change in productivity as a residual - i.e. the share of growth which is left after the contributions of capital and labor are taken out.

Provided that the shares of capital and labor in gross income are given (constant), the output growth rate depends on the growth rates of capital stock, employment and total factor productivity. The growth rate of capital is subject to approximation by means of the perpetual inventory method or the constant capital-output ratio approach. If we assume that these methods provide a relatively accurate assessment of capital accumulation, the only unexplained component in the growth accounting equation (Formula 2.4) remains the growth rate of total factor productivity (the so called Solow residual), which can be calculated as in Formula (2.5).

The growth accounting concept has been further elaborated by adding new factors to the production function and by relaxing its strict assumptions. Denison (1967) explained economic growth not only by the accumulation of production factors (capital, labor and land) but also by the way these resources were used and by the improvement in their qualities. The studies of Mankiw et al. (1992), Dougherty and Jorgenson (1996) and Hall and Jones (1996) emphasized the importance of human capital either as a separate factor or as a factor affecting the total factor productivity. Maddison (1982) stressed the necessity of making adjustments to the production factors in order to account for the improvement in their qualities.

Gradually the assumption of perfect competition has been abandoned and other variables such as market expansion and positive changes in resource allocation have been included in the production functions.

On the grounds of its characteristic features, the concept of growth accounting can be defined as a methodological approach to quantifying the contributions of main growth factors to economic growth in the long run. A merit of the growth accounting concept is that it can be easily applied in empirical studies. A shortcoming of growth accounting is the lack of analysis of the relationships between model variables and of the factors, which influence their dynamics.

In this monograph the impact of the changes in labor, physical capital and total factor productivity on the changes in real gross domestic product (GDP) has been investigated by means of the basic growth accounting equation (Formula 2.4). The way of defining the total factor productivity's contribution to economic growth (as a residual obtained by extracting from the output's growth rate the contributions of the two basic growth factors), gives the term "total factor productivity" a specific broader meaning. The dynamics of the total factor productivity reflects the influence of all sources of real GDP growth which are not changes in employment and in physical capital accumulation, such as research and development and the formation of human capital.

There are three methodological problems related to the practical application of the growth accounting technique:

1) How to estimate the elasticity coefficients in the production function;
2) How to measure labor input;
3) How to measure the growth rate of capital stock?

A basic assumption of the economic equilibrium theory is that each production factor is awarded its marginal productivity. The shares of capital $\boldsymbol{\alpha}$ and labor $\boldsymbol{\beta}$ in gross income (GDP) can be determined as $\boldsymbol{\alpha} = \mathbf{rK/Y}$ and $\boldsymbol{\beta} = \mathbf{wL/Y}$, where $\mathbf{r}$ is the real interest rate and $\mathbf{w}$ is the real wage. Hence, $\boldsymbol{\beta}$ is the share of labor income in GDP and $\boldsymbol{\alpha}$ is the share of capital income in GDP.

In the original version of the growth accounting technique $\boldsymbol{\beta}$ was set equal to $\mathbf{(1\text{-}\alpha)}$ in accordance with the assumption of constant returns to scale. However, in many recent empirical studies (Krueger, 1999; Senhadji, 2000; Ganev, 2005;

Tsalinski, 2007) **β** was determined as the share of compensation of employees in GDP, and **α** was obtained as **α = (1-β)**. The rationale of the new approach is that **α** ought to show the share of capital income in GDP, which can be calculated by dividing the sum of the net operating surplus and the net mixed income by GDP. However, defining **α** as a residual actually means that its value is increased by the share of the consumption of fixed capital in GDP and the difference between the shares of the net taxes on production and the financial intermediation services indirectly measured in GDP. Another reason for overvaluing **α** is the fact that a part of the net mixed income is in reality a labor income and should be added to the compensation of employees.

The original approach to calculating **α** and **β** and its contemporary modifications have their merits and demerits. This paper analyzes five equilibrium approaches to calculating elasticities in an attempt to find out which approach provides the most accurate and reliable estimates of elasticities in the production function.

The first equilibrium approach to estimating the elasticity coefficients was used by Minassian (2008) and is based on the final expenditure structure of GDP. According to this approach, the elasticity **α** is set equal to the share of gross capital formation (gross investment) in GDP and the elasticity **β** is set equal to the share of final consumption in GDP. A specificity of this approach is that GDP is calculated as a sum of final consumption and gross capital formation, while net exports are not included in the calculation. A consequence of this way of calculating GDP is that the sum of the elasticities **α** and **β** equals 1. If net exports were included in GDP calculation, then the sum of **α** and **β** would not equal 1.

According to the first approach **α** and **β** are calculated as follows:

$$\alpha = GCF/(GCF + FC) \qquad \textbf{(2.6)}$$

$$\beta = FC/(GCF + FC) \quad \textbf{(2.7)}$$

where:

GCF - gross capital formation;

FC - final consumption.

The values of the elasticities **α** and **β** obtained by the first approach are shown in Table 2.13.

Table 2.13. Elasticity coefficients obtained in accordance with the five equilibrium approaches

	First approach		Second approach		Third approach		Fourth approach		Fifth approach	
Year	α_1	β_1	α_2	β_2	α_3	β_3	α_4	β_4	α_5	β_5
1997	0,11	0,89	0,62	0,38	0,42	0,58	0,46	0,54	0,57	0,43
1998	0,17	0,83	0,54	0,46	0,36	0,64	0,44	0,56	0,47	0,53
1999	0,20	0,80	0,51	0,49	0,34	0,66	0,44	0,56	0,43	0,57
2000	0,19	0,81	0,54	0,46	0,36	0,64	0,44	0,56	0,47	0,53
2001	0,19	0,81	0,54	0,46	0,36	0,64	0,44	0,56	0,47	0,53
2002	0,20	0,80	0,55	0,45	0,36	0,64	0,46	0,54	0,47	0,53
2003	0,20	0,80	0,53	0,47	0,35	0,65	0,46	0,54	0,44	0,56
2004	0,21	0,79	0,53	0,47	0,35	0,65	0,46	0,54	0,44	0,56
2005	0,24	0,76	0,52	0,48	0,35	0,65	0,46	0,54	0,43	0,57
2006	0,27	0,73	0,53	0,47	0,35	0,65	0,46	0,54	0,44	0,56
2007	0,29	0,71	0,54	0,46	0,36	0,64	0,46	0,54	0,46	0,54
2008	0,31	0,69	0,53	0,47	0,35	0,65	0,44	0,56	0,46	0,54
2009	0,27	0,73	0,50	0,50	0,34	0,66	0,43	0,57	0,43	0,57
2010	0,23	0,77	0,48	0,52	0,32	0,68	0,43	0,57	0,40	0,60
2011	0,22	0,78	0,51	0,49	0,34	0,66	0,44	0,56	0,44	0,56
2012	0,22	0,78	0,49	0,51	0,33	0,67	0,42	0,58	0,42	0,58
2013	0,21	0,79	0,46	0,54	0,31	0,69	0,40	0,60	0,40	0,60
Average	0,22	0,78	0,52	0,48	0,35	0,65	0,44	0,56	0,45	0,55

Source: Own calculation on the basis of data from the website of the National Statistical Institute of Bulgaria www.nsi.bg

The second equilibrium approach to estimating the elasticity coefficients was used by Raleva (2013). It is based on the income structure of GDP and more precisely on the income from production factors, which is a sum of compensation of employees, net operating surplus and net mixed income. The coefficient **β** shows the share of compensation of employees in the income from production factors:

$$\beta = CE \div (CE + NOS + NMI) \quad \textbf{(2.8)}$$

where:
CE - compensation of employees;
NOS - net operating surplus;
NMI - net mixed income.

The coefficient **α** equals the share of the sum of net operating surplus and net mixed income in the income from production factors:

$$\alpha = (NOS + NMI) \div (CE + NOS + NMI) \quad \textbf{(2.9)}$$

The values of the elasticities **α** and **β** obtained by the second approach are shown in Table 2.13. Calculated in accordance with the second approach, the coefficients **α** and **β** are the real weights of the production factors in GDP. A shortcoming of the second approach is the overvaluation of the share of capital income and the undervaluation of the share of labor income, which arises from treating the whole net mixed income as capital income.

The third equilibrium approach to estimating the elasticity coefficients is a modification of the second approach and was also used by Raleva (2013). According to the third approach the whole net mixed income is treated as labor income. Labor income is calculated by adding to compensation of employees one third of the sum of net mixed income and net operating surplus. Capital income equals two thirds of the sum of net mixed income and net operating surplus. The coefficients **α** and **β** are calculated as

$$\alpha = \frac{2}{3}(NOS + NMI)/(CE + NOS + NMI) \quad \textbf{(2.10)}$$

$$\beta = [CE + 1/3\,(NOS + NMI)] \,/\, (CE + NOS + NMI) \quad \textbf{(2.11)}$$

The sum of α and β is 1. The values of α and β obtained according to the third approach are shown in Table 2.13.

A flaw of the third approach is the overvaluation of share of labor income (β) and the undervaluation of the share of capital income (α) since net mixed income does not consist entirely of labor income. Besides the property of overvaluing or undervaluing the real shares of labor income and capital income in GDP, the second and the third approaches to estimating α and β have another serious drawback. The calculated according to the second and the third approach coefficients α and β are not in fact GDP elasticities, because their calculation base includes only the income of production factors. However, if the calculation base were GDP, then the sum of α and β would not be 1.

The forth equilibrium approach was used by Raleva (2013). According to this approach, the coefficient β is calculated as the share of the sum of the compensation of employees and the net mixed income in GDP:

$$\beta = [\mathrm{CE} + \tfrac{1}{3}(\mathrm{NOS} + \mathrm{NMI})]/\mathrm{GDP} \qquad \textbf{(2.12)}$$

Assuming constant returns to scale, α is treated as a residual and equals **(1-β)**.

When the forth approach is applied, both α and β are overvalued. β is overvalued because in labor income is included the whole income of the non-corporate enterprises. α is overvalued because the other elements of the income structure of GDP are added to capital income. The values of α and β derived in accordance with the forth approach can be seen in Table 2.13.

The fifth equilibrium approach was used by Raleva (2013) and returns to the original model construction of the growth accounting concept. According to this approach, α is calculated first as

$$\alpha = (NOS + NMI)/GDP \qquad \textbf{(2.13)}$$

β is treated as a residual and equals **(1-α).** Capital income is obtained as a sum of net operating surplus and net mixed income, which leads to an overvaluation of **α** because net mixed income contains some labor income. **β** is overvalued too because of its residual character. The forth and the fifth approach restrict the distortion of the proportions between **α** and **β** caused by the different interpretation of net mixed income. The values of **α** and **β** derived in accordance with the fifth approach are shown in Table 2.13.

Two indicators can be used to measure labor input **L** in the production function - the number of employed persons or the number of hours worked in an economy. In this paper the first indicator is employed. The growth rates of the number of employed persons compared to the previous year are shown in Table 2.16.

The most complex methodological problem related to the practical application of the growth accounting approach is how to measure the growth rate of capital stock. Two different approaches can be used to solve this problem - the perpetual inventory method (Ganev, 2005) and the constant capital-output ratio approach (Minassian, 2008; Raleva, 2013). In this paper the constant capital-output ratio approach has been employed. According to this approach, the growth rate of capital **ΔK/K** depends on gross investment **I,** the rate of depreciation **d** and the value of capital stock **K** in the base period:

$$\Delta K/K = I/K - d \qquad \textbf{(2.14)}$$

I/K can be written as a proportion between the rate of accumulation **I/Y** and the capital-output ratio **K/Y:**

$$I/K = (I/Y)/(K/Y) \qquad \textbf{(2.15)}$$

If **I/K** is substituted in Formula (2.14) with the right-hand side of Equation (2.15), then growth rate of capital **ΔK/K** can be calculated as

$$\Delta K/K = (I/Y\ /\ K/Y) - d \qquad \textbf{(2.16)}$$

Like in many empirical investigations (Hernandez and Mauleon, 2003; Cororaton, 2002; Felipe, 1997 etc.), the assumed rate of depreciation **d** in this paper is 0.05.

The capital-output ratio **K/Y** is considered constant in economic theory. In empirical studies this ratio varies between 2 and 3. For Bulgaria the used values of the capital-output ratio are 2.5 (Minassian, 2008) and 2.3 (Raleva, 2013). For the purpose of this study the used value of the capital-output ratio 2.2. It has been calculated as the average gross-capital-formation-to-change-in-real-GDP ratio for the period 1998-2008 (in accordance with the assumption of Harrod and Domar that the average and the marginal productivity of capital are equal).

The growth rates of capital are shown in Table 2.16.

An OLS estimation of Bulgaria's aggregate production function

For the OLS estimation a two-factor Cobb-Douglas production function is employed:

$$Y = A*(K^\wedge\alpha)*(L^\wedge\beta)*(e^\wedge u\ ) \qquad \textbf{(2.17)}$$

where:

Y - real GDP;
A - total factor productivity (TFP);
K - capital stock;
L - labor input;
α - elasticity of GDP with respect to capital;

β - elasticity of GDP with respect to labor;
u - error term.

The Function (2.17) has been linearized by a logarithmic transformation:

$$\ln Y = \ln A + \alpha^* \ln K + \beta^* \ln L + u \qquad \textbf{(2.18)}$$

The OLS estimation of Bulgaria's aggregate production function has been performed in two variants - with annual data and with quarterly data.

OLS estimation with annual data

The first variant of the OLS estimation of Bulgaria's aggregate production function uses annual data of the National Statistical Institute of Bulgaria for real GDP (at prices of 2010), for real gross fixed capital formation (at prices of 2010) and for the number of employed persons for the period 1996-2014.

The results from estimating Equation (2.18) with annual data are shown in Table 2.14. Because of the small number of observations (19) the OLS estimation of the production function with annual data should be treated with caution and is made solely for the purpose of comparing its results with the results from the OLS estimation with quarterly data and with the results from GA.

At the 5% level, the elasticity coefficients **α** and **β** are statistically significant, but the intercept (total factor productivity **A)** is not. The estimated value of **α** (0.254070) indicates that a 1% change in gross fixed capital formation will cause a 0.25% change in GDP in the same direction, provided that the number of employed persons is held constant. The estimated value of **β** (0.985005) means that a 1% change in the number of employed persons will lead to a 0.99% change in

GDP in the same direction, if gross fixed capital formation remains unchanged. The OLS estimator of **α** obtained with annual data (0.25) is close to the average value of **α**, obtained via the first equilibrium approach (0.22). However, the OLS estimator of **β** o obtained with annual data (0.99) differs significantly from the average value of **β** derived via the first equilibrium approach (0.78). The OLS estimators of **α** and **β** obtained with annual data are higher than the average values of **α** and **β** calculated in accordance with the first equilibrium approach.

Table 2.14. Results from the OLS estimation of Bulgaria's aggregate production function for the period 1996-2014 with annual data

Variable	Coefficient	Standard error	t-statistic	Probability
ln A	0.609769	3.232859	0.188616	0.8528
Α	0.254070	0.034093	7.452281	0.0000
Β	0.985005	0.408935	2.408707	0.0284

Source: Own calculation on the basis of data from the website of the National Statistical Institute of Bulgaria www.nsi.bg

The coefficient of determination (R^2 = 0.842440) shows that 84.24% of changes in GDP during the period of investigation can be explained by changes in gross fixed capital formation and the number of employed persons. The probability of the F-statistic (0) indicates that at the 5% level of significance the alternative hypothesis for the adequacy of the regression model is accepted. The acceptance of the alternative hypothesis does not mean that the model specification is the best possible but only that the regression model adequately reflects the relationship between dependent variable and independent variables.

The value of 0.32 of the Durbin-Watson statistic presumes the existence of serial correlation (autocorrelation) of residuals. At the 5% level of significance the serial correlation LM test confirms the alternative hypothesis that residuals are serially correlated. The serial correlation of residuals is not unusual for time-series data. In the presence of serial correlation OLS estimates and based on them forecasts are inefficient but still unbiased and consistent. Since the regression model will not be used for forecasting, the serial correlation has not been removed from the model.

The residual heteroscedasticity test (Breusch-Pagan-Godfrey) confirms the null hypothesis for the absence of heteroscedasticity at the 5% level of significance.

The residual normality test (Jarque-Bera) confirms the null hypothesis for the presence of normal distribution of residuals at the 5% level of significance.

The estimated regression equation is

$$Y = 1.84 * (K\text{^}0.25) * (L\text{^}0.99) \qquad \textbf{(2.19)}$$

Since both **α** and **β** are less than one, GDP is non-elastic to both gross fixed capital formation and the number of employed persons.

The Wald test confirms the null hypothesis that **α+β=1** at the 5% level of significance. This agrees with the assumption of constant returns to scale of the neoclassical growth theory.

OLS estimation with quarterly data

The second variant of the OLS estimation of Bulgaria's aggregate production function employs quarterly seasonally adjusted data of the National Statistical Institute of Bulgaria for real GDP (at prices of 2010), for real gross fixed capital formation (at prices of 2010) and for the number of employed persons for the period from the first quarter of 1996 to the fourth quarter of 2014.

The performed Augmented Dickey-Fuller Unit Root Tests produced the following results:

- Log values of real GDP and their first differences are not stationary, but their second differences are stationary;

- Log values of real gross fixed capital formation are stationary;
- Log values of the number of employed persons and their first differences are not stationary, but their second differences are stationary.

In order to make the time series stationary, Equation (2.18) has been modified by using the second differences of log values of variables:

$$\ln Y_t - \ln Y_{t-2} = \ln A + \alpha * (\ln K_t - \ln K_{t-2}) + \beta * (\ln L_t - \ln L_{t-2}) + u \qquad \textbf{(2.20)}$$

The results from estimating Equation (2.20) are displayed in Table 2.15.

Table 2.15. Results from the OLS estimation of Bulgaria's aggregate production function for the period 1996-2014 with quarterly data

Variable	Coefficient	Standard error	t-statistic	Probability
ln A	0.000242	0.019729	0.012242	0.9903
A	0.219426	0.023909	9.177619	0.0000
B	0.390322	0.230159	1.695884	0.0944

Source: Own calculation on the basis of data from the website of the National Statistical Institute of Bulgaria www.nsi.bg

At the 5% level, the elasticity coefficient **α** is statistically significant, but the elasticity coefficient **β** and the intercept (total factor productivity **A)** are not. At the 10% level **β** becomes statistically significant. The estimated value of **α** (0.219426) indicates that a 1% change in gross fixed capital formation will cause a 0.22% change in GDP in the same direction, provided that the number of employed persons is held constant. The estimated value of **β** (0.390322**)** means that a 1% change in the number of employed persons will lead to a 0.39% change in GDP in the same direction, if gross fixed capital formation remains unchanged. The OLS estimator of **α** obtained with quarterly data (0.22) coincides with the average value of **α** calculated according to the first equilibrium approach (0.22). However, the OLS estimator of **β** obtained with quarterly data (0.39) is significantly higher than the average value of **β** derived in accordance with the first equilibrium approach (0.78).

The coefficient of determination (R^2 = 0.570997) shows that 57.1% of changes in GDP during the period of investigation can be explained by changes in gross fixed capital formation and the number of employed persons. The probability of the F-statistic (0) indicates that at the 5% level of significance the alternative hypothesis for the adequacy of the regression model is accepted. The acceptance of the alternative hypothesis does not mean that the model specification is the best possible but only that the regression model adequately reflects the relationship between dependent variable and independent variables.

The value of 2.79 the Durbin-Watson statistic presumes the existence of serial correlation (autocorrelation) of residuals. At the 5% level of significance the serial correlation LM test confirms the alternative hypothesis that residuals are serially correlated. The serial correlation of residuals is not unusual for time-series data. In the presence of serial correlation OLS estimates and based on them forecasts are inefficient but still unbiased and consistent. Since the regression model will not be used for forecasting, the serial correlation has not been removed from the model.

The residual heteroscedasticity test (ARCH) confirms the null hypothesis for the absence of heteroscedasticity at the 5% level of significance.

The residual normality test (Jarque-Bera) confirms the null hypothesis for the presence of normal distribution of residuals at the 5% level of significance.

Since **A = 1**, the estimated regression equation is

$$Y = (K^{0.22}) * (L^{0.39}) \quad \textbf{(2.21)}$$

Since both **α** and **β** are less than one, GDP is non-elastic to both gross fixed capital formation and the number of employed persons.

The Wald test confirms the null hypothesis that **α+β=1** at the 1% level of significance. This agrees with the assumption of constant returns to scale of the neoclassical growth theory.

Results from the growth accounting of Bulgaria

The values of the elasticities **α** and **β** obtained through the five equilibrium approaches can be seen in Table 2.13. The comparison with the OLS procedure results (see Tables 2.14 and 2.15) suggests that the first equilibrium approach provides the most accurate and reliable estimates of the elasticities **α** and **β** in Bulgaria's aggregate production function. Therefore, the first equilibrium approach has been used in the implementation of the growth accounting technique to Bulgaria.

The calculated results for the contributions of capital, labor and total factor productivity to economic growth in Bulgaria via the first equilibrium approach are displayed in Table 2.16.

Table 2.16. Contributions of capital, labor and total factor productivity to economic growth in Bulgaria in accordance with the first equilibrium approach

Year	ΔY/Y	α	ΔK/K	α*ΔK/K	β	ΔL/L	β*ΔL/L	ΔA/A
1997	-1.09%	0.11	-0.80%	-0.09%	0.89	-3.07%	-2.74%	1.74%
1998	3.46%	0.17	0.53%	0.09%	0.83	-1.03%	-0.85%	4.22%
1999	-5.65%	0.20	3.48%	0.70%	0.80	-4.32%	-3.45%	-2.90%
2000	6.04%	0.19	3.05%	0.57%	0.81	-2.38%	-1.93%	7.40%
2001	3.80%	0.19	3.67%	0.71%	0.81	-0.75%	-0.61%	3.70%
2002	4.48%	0.20	3.94%	0.78%	0.80	0.23%	0.18%	3.52%
2003	5.36%	0.20	4.23%	0.86%	0.80	2.96%	2.36%	2.14%
2004	6.56%	0.21	4.58%	0.96%	0.79	2.59%	2.05%	3.55%
2005	5.96%	0.24	6.44%	1.54%	0.76	2.70%	2.05%	2.36%
2006	6.47%	0.27	7.55%	2.01%	0.73	3.34%	2.45%	2.01%
2007	6.91%	0.29	8.41%	2.40%	0.71	3.18%	2.27%	2.24%
2008	5.75%	0.31	10.0%	3.13%	0.69	2.36%	1.62%	1.00%
2009	-5.01%	0.27	8.26%	2.22%	0.73	-1.71%	-1.25%	-5.98%
2010	0.66%	0.23	5.61%	1.30%	0.77	-3.88%	-2.98%	2.33%
2011	1.98%	0.22	4.73%	1.02%	0.78	-2.20%	-1.72%	2.68%
2012	0.49%	0.22	4.83%	1.06%	0.78	-2.50%	-1.95%	1.38%
2013	1.07%	0.21	4.70%	1.01%	0.79	-0.43%	-0.34%	0.40%
Average	2.78%	0.22	4.90%	1.19%	0.78	-0.29%	-0.29%	1.87%
St. Dev.	3.80%	4.59%	2.66%	0.81%	4.59%	2.58%	2.00%	2.81%

Source: Own calculation on the basis of data from the website of the National Statistical Institute of Bulgaria www.nsi.bg

As a whole the dynamics of Bulgaria's output under a CBA has been positive (see Table 2.16). For the entire period 1997-2013 the real GDP of Bulgaria decreased in three years only – in 1997, 1997 and 2009. However, the average growth rate for the whole period is not high - 2.78%. The standard deviation of growth rates of 3.8% implies that Bulgaria's economic growth under a CBA has been unstable and uneven. In 1997 the fall in real output was small (1.09%) but in 1999 and in 2009 it was disastrous (5.65% and 5.01% respectively). The main contributor to the serious drop in real GDP in 1999 was employment (with a fall of 3.45%) and in 2009 - total factor productivity (with a fall of 5.98%).

The period 2000-2008 was characterized by a relatively high and steady economic growth with an average rate of

5.70% and a standard deviation of 1.01%. In the first part of this period (from 2000 till 2004) the total factor productivity was the main driving force of growth with an average contribution of 4.06%. However, in the second part of the period (from 2005 till 2008) the growth of real GDP was determined mostly by changes in capital stock, whose average contribution was 2.27%.

After the collapse in 2009 (a 5% decline in real output) the recovery of Bulgarian economy has been slow and weak. In the years 2010-2013 Bulgaria recorded a faint economic growth of less than 2% per annum and 1.05% on average. This weak growth has been determined mainly by negative changes in employment (an average drop of 1.75%).

The total factor productivity (with a standard deviation of 2.81%) has been the most volatile of the three growth determinants. Capital stock (with a standard deviation of 0.81%) has been the most stable contributor to Bulgaria's economic growth under a CBA.

The contribution of labor to economic growth was positive in 2002-2008 but negative in 1997-2001 and 2009-2013. The average contribution of employment to economic growth for the whole period 1997-2013 is negative (-0.29%). The comparison of the dynamics of output and employment demonstrates that positive changes in the labor market occurred after two years of high and steady economic growth. However, the response of labor market to poor output developments has been immediate.

The fluctuations of output and the total factor productivity show similar patterns. This fact is due to the specificity of the calculation of the change in total factor productivity as a residual obtained from the growth rate of output by subtracting the growth rates of capital stock and labor input.

The contribution of changes in capital stock to economic growth was positive in all years of the period 1997-2013 except for the year 1997, when it was negative. The average contribution of capital stock to economic growth for the period 1997-2013 is 1.19%, which makes it the second largest contributor to Bulgaria's economic growth under a CBA after TFP (with an average contribution of 1.87%). The peak contributions of changes in capital stock to economic growth were in the years 2003-2008 (an average of 1.82%). After the upward movements in 1997-2008, the impact of capital stock on economic growth decreased in 2009-2013 (an average of 1.32%, or a decline of 0.5% compared to the period 2003-2008). It may be inferred that the increase in capital stock in 1997-2008 resulted from an improvement of the business environment in Bulgaria. This improvement of the business environment was caused by the following events:

- The introduction of the CBA in 1997, which led to financial and macroeconomic stability;
- The increase in lending in 2003-2008, which was due to the purchase of Bulgarian banks by foreign banks and to the massive inflow of foreign capital to Bulgaria;
- The accession of Bulgaria to the European Union, which increased the certainty for foreign investors in Bulgaria.

As a result of the global and domestic economic crisis and the slow recovery of Bulgarian economy from this crisis, the influence of changes in capital stock on economic growth fell in 2009-2013, when the uncertain political and economic environment led to a sharp drop in investment.

It can be concluded that total factor productivity and capital stock have been the main supply-side determinants of economic growth in Bulgaria under a CBA while the influence of changes in employment on the dynamics of real GDP has been weaker. The dynamics of total factor productivity under a CBA has been rather chaotic, which may be attributed to the inconsistent development of the transition to a market-oriented economy in Bulgaria. The ineffective use of labor resources has contributed to lowering the growth rates of real GDP. This small negative impact of employment has been offset by rises in total factor productivity and capital stock. The decline in employment has been accompanied by increased influence of scientific progress and organizational factors. Economic effectiveness has increased in the process of privatization and restructuring of the Bulgarian economy.

https://doi.org/10.2478/9783110619218-004

CHAPTER. THE CYCLICAL RECURRENCE OF THE BULGARIAN ECONOMY

3.1. Theoretical background

Cyclicality exists everywhere around us. There is a change in the annual seasons and the everyday life of the people. Examples for cyclicality can be found in the history of mankind and the planet as a whole. Cyclical economy has been observed since ancient times. There is an alternation of economic crises and economic growth in Greece, the Roman Empire, Egypt and other ancient countries.

The business cycle is conditioned by the economic activity of society. It impacts on countries' economic policies, the business plans of different companies, and household spending plans.

Business cycles represent an alternation of periods of upward and downward economic activity. The study of business cycle developed in the period after the Industrial Revolution, as the business cycle required the existence of sufficient trade relationships. '... in the pre-industrial societies, crises are mainly the result of natural disasters, cycles of agricultural production, wars, disease outbreaks, etc. ... in the era of industrialization, the main factors influencing the fluctuations in aggregate production, prices, etc., are largely related to and derive from the economic activity of people and the peculiarities

of the economic organization of society '(Ganev, 2015, p.2). In pre-industrial society, crises are of no economic interest because of their nature. If an event or phenomenon is of a one-time nature and there are no signs of its manifestation in a future period, it is likely to be missed or given little attention by the scientific community. Another significant reason is the lack of sufficient quantitative and qualitative data.

The study of the business cycle began in the 18-19th century. At first, due to the economists' understanding of that time, only the crises and their causes were considered and described. Only after years of accumulation of information, the study of periods of economic expansion started. There is a need for broad and deep monitoring of the rapidly industrializing economies in order to identify cyclical changes in the development of production. Gathering a sufficiently large volume of information requires much time. Systematic historical and statistical observations are necessary for the discovery of regularity.

Determining the business cycle requires the availability of a set of metrics. The changes in their values are considered to be a clear indicator of changes in economic dynamics over a period that can coincide with the assumed business cycle. In order to prove the existence of the business cycle, the repetition of phenomena that characterize the changes in the set of indicators and the changes in the economic dynamics must be established. Once the set of specific indicators is defined and sufficient statistical information is gathered, a quantitative and qualitative analysis of the phenomenon that is selected for observation can be made, i.e. the business cycle.

There is no commonly accepted definition of 'business cycle' in economic literature. Individual authors offer different definitions that overlap. According to Carlgren (2015), the business cycle is defined as the fluctuations of the average economic activity that moves in a cyclical pattern with varying frequency and amplitude. It has two turning points (top and bottom) and two phases (expansion and recession) that are connected to each other. Burns and Mitchell (1946) define business cycles as '... a type of fluctuations inherent in the aggregate economic activity of nations that organize their work mainly in business enterprises: a cycle consists of expansions occurring at about the same time in many economic activities, followed by similarly general recessions, contractions, and revivals which merge into the expansion phase of the next cycle; in duration, business cycles vary from more than one year to ten or twelve years; they are not divisible into shorter cycles of similar characteristics with amplitudes approximating their own.'

The business cycle covers the entire economy, not just individual sectors. It is a macroeconomic phenomenon that affects the whole of society. For this reason, it is subject to the economic policy of the state. Its very name implies that the business cycle is not a random one-time occurrence, but a periodically recurring phenomenon. The difficulty in predicting it is due to its variable amplitude and duration. The adaptation to the economic cycle is complex. Accor-ding to Burns and Mitchell's definition, the business cycle differs from other periodically recurring business phenomena.

Events that last less than one year are not part of the business cycle, they are considered seasonal fluctuations. They are not part of the business cycle of phenomena that last over ten or twelve years (the so-called 'growth cycles' or 'Kuznets cycles'). They last for 15-25 years and are due to demographic dynamics of the population and investments in infrastructure, as well as the 'long waves'. The latter are also known as 'Kondratiev cycles', lasting from 40 to 60 years, and are associated with technological advances, population dynamics, credit cycles, debt burden, and so on.

According to the Fourier Theorem, each periodic function can be represented as a combination of simple periodic functions. Each economic cycle consists of smaller business cycles. There are several basic types of economic cycles, and the main difference between them is their duration. After excluding phenomena lasting less than one year due to their seasonal nature, there are basically three types of cycles: long waves, economic growth cycles, and short-term business cycles.

Economic growth is defined as a long-term process in which, over a long period of time, there is a real increase in the level of the aggregate product. According to Kuznets (1971, p. 1), 'a country's economic growth can be defined as a long-term increase in the capacity to offer the population more and more diverse economic assets; this growing capacity is based on the advances in technology and the required institutional and ideological adaptation.' The long-term upward trend of economic growth is the result of growing production opportunities.

It is possible for the long-term trend of the economy to be downward. 'It may result from a series of subsequent lower maximum (peak) and minimum (bottom) GDP growth rates over the period covered. Thus, the downward trend may be a reflected result of the increased absolute parameters and economies of scale in which the relative expressions of the observed growth may be smaller or decreasing', Pirimova (2014, p. 26) The long-term economic cycle tracks the results of the development of various processes whose effects become visible when observing longer periods of time, namely, population growth, efficiency of production factors, the emergence of new markets and new sources of raw materials, structural transformations in the economy, and others.

Short-term economic cycles reflect the monthly, quarterly or annual economic circumstances, depending on the time interval analyzed. There is the possibility that real GDP may change at different rates - positive, negative or zero. With short-term economic cycles, the trend may be formed in different directions. It may be ascending or descending, or horizontal. This distinguishes it from the long-term one, which is usually unidirectional and ascending. The trend follows the changes in the growth rate of GDP as well as the fluctuation intensity.

Long waves or the so-called Kondratiev cycles bear the name of their discoverer (Garvy, 1943). In his studies,

Kondratiev discovers the existence of fluctuations in economic activity lasting from 40 to 60 years which arise from technological advances, population dynamics, various social cataclysms, credit cycles, the debt burden, the renewal of capital goods, and others.

The theory of long waves is not accepted by the majority of economists, but is gaining popularity and is used for studying the economy in the past as well as analyzing the stock markets.

The name 'long waves' originates from their graphic representation which resembles waves. Kondratiev divides each cycle into four phases - prosperity, recession, depression and improvement (Kondratiev, 1935). Literature may also include a three-phase division of Kondratiev cycles – stagnation, recession and expansion. Kondratiev made his conclusions based on the study of a huge amount of statistical information on the interest rate, nominal wages, prices, and the foreign trade turnover of developed countries for the period from the end of the 18th century to 1920.

According to Kondratiev, long waves are caused by crises emerging in cases where the outdated economic structure is contrary to modern technologies and the new, more efficient organization of production. The inability to make the necessary changes in the structure of the economy leads to a slow and painful change that results in a slowdown in economic development and production stagnation. It is only after the inconsistencies between the economic structure and the new technologies have been overcome that there is a revival and the conditions for the conjunctural development are improved. An important role for entering the upward part of the cycle play the changes in the policy area (the creation of new countries or the outbreak of revolutions) and the improvement of the conditions for the development of the economy (the penetration of new inventions, improvements in scientific and technological progress and the optimization of the productive activity).

According to Schumpeter (1939), the causes of long waves are rooted in the wavy development of technical and technological innovation. Every major technological breakthrough gives new opportunities for capital investment. Accumulation of innovations which takes place under certain conditions, leads to the formation of the upward part of the cycle. The rate of profitability and return increases, which results in the accumulation of capital. Over time, market saturation occurs, and the realization of new production is hampered by declining aggregate demand. The result is a shrinking of production and a drop in the profit rate. The accumulated capital cannot be realized, and it becomes redundant, which gives rise to the downward phase of the cycle, the outcome of which is the next technological breakthrough.

Kondratiev cycles and Kuznets cycles are considered long-term cycles in economic science. Kuznets cycles are called cycles of economic growth because Kuznets analyses the link between the rate of economic growth and the changes in the leading industries in the economy (Kuznets, 1930). The duration of the Kuznets cycles is between 15 and 25 years, the major factors for them to occur being the changes in housing, demographic change and infrastructure investment. The Kuznets Cycles have three phases (Kuznets, 1929):

- first phase - prosperity lasting from 3 to 6 years;
- second phase - stable full-time growth of 7 to 11 years;
- third phase - depression or stagnation lasting from 4 to 7 years, with the level of unemployment being high throughout almost the entire period of the phase.

Two types of short-term cycles are known in the economic science. These are the Kitchin cycles (lasting between 3 and 5 years) and the Juglar cycles (lasting between 7 and 11 years).

Kitchin's cycle is caused by changes in available stocks (Kitchin, 1923). It is associated with time lags in information movements affecting the decision making of commercial firms. Companies respond to the improvement of the commercial situation by increasing production through full employment of the production capital. Within a certain period (ranging between a few months to two years) - the market gets 'flooded' with commodities. The decline in demand and prices, and the accumulation of produced commodities force entrepreneurs to reduce output. This process takes some time because of the time lags in information movements from the market to the business representatives. It takes time for entrepreneurs to analyze the obtained market information and decide on their future actions. The very materialization of the decision made also takes time. It is exactly these time lags that give rise to Kitchin's cycle. Once the decision to reduce production is implemented and the market gets back to normal, conditions are beginning to be observed for the start of a new upward phase of demand, prices and output, i.e. of the cycle itself.

Within the Juglar cycle, fluctuations in fixed capital investment can be observed, and not just changes in the level of fixed capital and the stock levels, as it is in the Kitchin cycle (Juglar,1862). Often, the Juglar cycle is defined as the main economic cycle.

Kitchin, Juglar, and Burns and Mitchell cycles have a duration of three to seven years and meet the business cycle definition.

There are two alternative types of business cycles caused by the ability of the economic situation to be variable and divergent - irregular fluctuations in growth and economic growth cycles. These varieties of the short-term economic cycle can alternate and exist within a longer cycle (Pirimova, 2014, p. 28). Irregular fluctuations in growth are caused by the volatility of the growth rate of GDP, by chaotic, consistent and frequent changes in its level.

On the other hand, the economic growth cycles arise from a relatively regular, non-chaotic and periodically recurring wave change in the growth rate of aggregate production over several years. During this period there is a slowing of growth and a shift towards its acceleration or vice versa.

Economic cycles have several characteristics that occur in all types. An important feature of business cycles is that they are synchronous. This means that they do not cause changes in an industry or a sector but are predominant in nature. Depression occurs in all industries and sectors of the economy at the same time. The recession is shifting from one industry to another, and this chain reaction continues until the entire economy is affected. Similar is the process of growth. Prosperity is spread through the various input-output links or through the relationships between the different sectors and industries of the economy.

The types of cycles are determined by their duration, and the first of their characteristic is their intensity. When economic growth is positive, its rate may be rising, falling or remaining relatively stable. When the growth rate of real GDP is positive and higher than the growth rate for the previous year, there is expansion of growth. Where there is a decline in the positive real GDP growth rate compared to the previous year, there is a slowdown or growth recession. Growth stagnation occurs when the realized economic growth has approximately the same, usually relatively low growth rates of real GDP. This also applies to periods when the level of GDP remains stable, i.e. when there is zero real GDP growth. The duration of the periods in which these processes take place may be different. There is also the possibility that 'the dynamics of growth is stable - carried out with successively increasing rates, or unstable - accompanied by some more frequent fluctuations and transitions between the three processes of acceleration, slowing down and growth retardation, or wavy (cyclic). '(Pirimova, 2014, p. 28). The same processes can also occur in the case of a negative trend of real GDP growth.

An important characteristic of the cycles is their phases. With the Kondratiev's cycles, four phases are distinguished - prosperity, recession, depression and improvement, and in economic literature a three-phase division of the 'long waves' can be found - stagnation, recession and expansion. Kuznets cycles are divided into three stages - expansion after depression (lasting between 4-6 years), steady growth at full employment (between 7 and 11 years), and stagnation or depression with high unemployment (lasting between 4 and 7 years). Short-term cycles have two phases - a phase of expansion that ends at a peak, and a phase of recession that ends at the bottom.

Cycle dynamics is measured by real GDP growth, with the turning points (tops and bottoms) being plotted graphically as the highest and lowest points, above or below the flat trend line and the abscissa. Depending on the nature of the changes, especially at the bottom, the graphical images of the economic cycles can take V-shaped, W-shaped and U-shaped forms. The L-shaped and J-shaped formations are much less common, respectively in the phase of contraction and the growth phase.

It is typical of V-shaped economic cycles that only one bottom is formed within their borders, after which the conditions for growth of the economy are restored and it again enters the expansion phase.

W-shaped economic cycles form two bottoms due to stronger recessionary tendencies that are more difficult to overcome. The first bottom is followed by a short-term, usually one-year increase in real GDP, with a subsequent second decline in the indicator. A lasting trend of growth and recovery only occurs after the second bottom is passed.

U-shaped economic cycles are characterized by protracted periods of crisis turbulence and depressive state of the economy. There are several years of absolute downturns of close relative value, with the bottom period being smooth and prolonged.

The L-shape is formed in a recessionary phase, and it is characterized by the fact that after a large decline in the economy over a long period there is little or no growth possibly followed by years of stagnation, such as the situation in Japan over the 90s.

The J-shape is due to a slight decline in economic growth as a result of reforms that later on lead to strong and sustained productivity growth.

According to various economics schools, the cause of business cycles can be searched in various places. According to the classical school, a business cycle cannot exist because imbalances are quickly overcome by changes in prices and wages. 'Classical economists claim that prices and wages adapt rapidly to changes in supply or demand' (Todorov, Iv., 2016, p.). 'This opinion suggests that shocks in aggregate demand only have a short effect on actual variables such as real GDP' (Ibid., p. 84).

The early theories of the business cycle assume that over a long period of time aggregate production may deviate from the level that corresponds to full employment in the economy. These early theories focus on the causes of fluctuations and on the occurrence of crises, and not on the cyclical development of the economy as a whole.

William. S. Jevons assumes that changes in solar activity are the cause of cycles (Jevons, W. S., 1884), and according to Henry Moore, economic crises are caused by climate changes (Moore, H. L. 1914). John Mills does not accept the assumption that economic cycles are caused by economic factors. He thinks that the main cause of crises lies in the human factor, namely the human psyche, and it is the loss of belief in value (Mills, J., 1868). Arthur Pigou also considers psychological factors as the main cause of economic cycles. In his theory, the mood of investors and entrepreneurs is the main driving force of cyclicality. Pigou describes investors' behavior as that of a herd, as it is guided by the moods of the group (Pigou, A. C., 1923).

According to the Swiss economist Jean-Charles Sismondi, the cause of the crises is endogenous and is in production that remains unrealized, i.e., the so-called overproduction, which is a loss for investors because these are costs against which no revenue is generated (De Sismondi, J.-C.-L., 1819). Thomas Malthus points out the two-way dependence between demographic cyclicality and production cycles as a cause of the business cycle. The more the population grows, the more the poverty and the shortage increase (Malthus, T. 1798).

Gustav Kassel, the representative of the Stockholm School of Economics, describes the economic cycles initially as changes in production, subsequently, their influence on the factors of production, especially on their dynamics, then on price and income fluctuations, and finally, on the dynamics of capital markets. According to Kassel, economic cycles have an endogenous character and their cause is rooted in processes and factors on the economy and those that are the product of human behavior (Cassel, G. 1967).

According to the Austrian economist Josef Schumpeter, cyclicality in the economy can be triggered by a number of exogenous and endogenous factors for the economy. Schumpeter considers only the internal factors for the emergence of economic cycles due to the fact that external factors are not of an economic nature. He systematizes endogenous factors into three groups:

- Changes in preferences - utility functions of consumers change;
- Changes in the quantity of factors of production - this group includes the increase in labor force and investments;
- Changes in the methods of offering products - this group includes the introduction of new technologies, the opening of new markets, etc. (Schumpeter, 1939).

For the famous Swedish economist and founder of Stockholm School of Economics, Knut Wicksell, crises and macroeconomic fluctuations are casual, and they cannot be a cycle.

Wicksell defined as causes of macroeconomic fluctuations '... external circumstances belonging to economic life ... and partly ... the internal structure of the economy viewed from a material and psychological stand-point, namely the period of time necessary for completing large economic undertakings, and the time that is required before a general, optimistic outlook on the market is changed to a pessimistic one, and vice versa '(Wicksell, K. 1953 [1907] p. 224).

The representatives of the Austrian School of Economics assume the cause of business cycles lies in the natural interest rate and the deviations from it. According to Ludwig von Mises, the increase in the amount of money in circulation leads to changes in the natural interest rate, which generates cyclical fluctuations (Mises, L., 1953). Friedrich Hayek adds the role of monetary authorities to the analysis and more precisely, the uncontrolled printing of money by the central bank (Hayek, F. A. (1935 [1931]).

John Maynard Keynes determines the marginal efficiency of capital, a specific type of interest rate introduced by him, as the main factor generating cyclical fluctuations. As a result of a sudden loss of confidence that cannot be accurately determined, there is a crisis leading to a collapse in the values of that factor. The other two psychological factors - the liquidity preference and the marginal propensity to consume - are simply additional circumstances complicating the situation as a consequence of the increase in the interest rate and the decline in consumption (Keynes, J.M., 1993)

Unlike the Keynesians, monetarists assume that the fluctuations in the economy are caused by changes in the amount of money, and the reason for the increase of the amplitudes of the business cycle is rooted in the erroneous expectations and slow adaptation of economic agents to the changes in the economic environment. Milton Friedman's views differ from those of the early monetarists. According to Friedman, money supply as an aggregate macroeconomic magnitude rather than credit is the basis of fluctuations. Friedman's theory is also contrary to Keynesian theory, according to which investment and generally real factors are the cause of fluctuations in the economy (Friedman, M. and Schwartz, A., 1965).

The representative of rational expectations school, Robert Lucas, views the business cycle as an erroneous expectation of economic agents about relative prices. Economic agents mistakenly assess changes in price levels, confusing them with changes in relative prices, and therefore make changes in their own production (Lucas, R.E., 1973).

According to Kydland and Prescott, the initial impulses of the business cycle arise from the development of technology, and the need for a long period of time to build up production capacities acts as a mechanism for distribution of cycles and amplifies cyclical fluctuations (Kydland, F. E., and Prescott, E. C., 1988).

According to the new Keynesian theory, prices and wages are inflexible. In the short term, money and monetary policy are not neutral and there is monopoly competition (Gali, J., 2008). These peculiarities lead to a strengthening of fluctuations in the short and medium term and are an obstacle to the rapid restoration of balance. They create inefficiency. Therefore, from a dynamic perspective, the business cycle is an inefficient state of the economy. The lack of money neutrality in the short term is the main impetus that leads to the generation of fluctuations in the economic system.

Stanley Fisher agrees with neo-classics that the change in the amount of money is the cause of business cycles. Instead of the forecast errors made by economic agents, he accepts long-term contracts relating to certain nominal variables (wages) as the main cause of the long-term mismatch of real variables from their equilibrium states due to money impulses (Fischer, S., 1977). According to Christiano, Eichenbaum and Evans, fluctuations in aggregate production and inflation, which are inherent in the business cycle, are caused by monetary shocks (Christiano, L., Eichenbaum, M. and Evans, C., 2005).

The conclusions that can be drawn from the study of Richard Clarida, Jordi Gali and Mark Gertler, which is fundamental to the New Keynesian models, are that both demand and supply factors can be an impulse to generate business cycles, and many of these factors can be identified as shocks. Also, for the better impact of economic policy on economic fluctuations, it is necessary to have a better knowledge of the processes taking place in a given economy as the economic policy potential for stabilizing production and inflation around their equilibrium level is not reached. The third conclusion which can be reached is that the current knowledge does not allow short term stabilization of the production and inflation via economic policy instruments (Clarida, R., Gali, J. and Gertler, M., 1999).

Macroeconomic theory has to go a long way to be able to give a satisfactory explanation of the cycle. At present, the New Keynesian models are the best alternative to allow both forecasting and analyzing macroeconomic indicators and assessing economic policy options, taking into account their combination of empirical feasibility and theoretical endurance.

3.2. Estimating Bulgaria's potential output and determining the cyclical position of the Bulgarian economy

Assumptions and methodology of calculations

As in Gladnishki (2005), in this research Bulgaria's potential output is estimated by a methodology based on a two-factor Cobb-Douglas production function:

$$(3.1)\ \mathbf{YPOT = A * K^{\alpha} * LPOT^{\beta}}$$

where **YPOT** is Bulgaria's potential output, **A** is total factor productivity, **K** is capital stock, **α** is the elasticity of output with respect to capital, **LPOT** is the potential (optimal) employment of labor resources and **β** is the elasticity of output with respect to labor.

The elasticity coefficients are estimated via an equilibrium approach, which is based on the income structure of Bulgaria's GDP and was used by Raleva (2013). According to this approach the whole mixed income is treated as a labor income. The labor income is calculated by adding to the compensation of employees **CE** one third of the sum of the net mixed income **NMI** and the net operating surplus **NOS**. The capital income equals two thirds of the sum of the net mixed income **NMI** and the net operating surplus **NOS**. The coefficients **α** and **β** are calculated as

$$(3.2)\ \alpha = \frac{2}{3}(NOS + NMI)/(CE + NOS + NMI)$$

$$(3.3)\ \beta = [CE + 1/3\,(NOS + NMI)]\,/\,(CE + NOS + NMI)$$

The sum of **α** and **β** is 1. The average values of **α** and **β** for the period 1997-2015 are respectively 0.35 and 0.65 and are used in estimating Bulgaria's potential output.

Since the Bulgarian national statistics does not provide data on capital stock, one of the methodological problems, related to potential output estimation, is how to calculate the size of capital stock. Two approaches can be used to solve this problem – the perpetual inventory method (Ganev, 2005) and the constant capital-output ratio approach (Minassian, 2008; Raleva, 2013; Todorov, 2015). In this monograph the constant capital-output ratio approach is employed.

The capital-output ratio **K/Y** is considered constant in economic theory. In empirical studies this ratio varies between 2 and 3. For Bulgaria the used values of the capital-output ratio are 2.5 (Minassian, 2008), 2.3 (Raleva, 2013) and 2.2 (Todorov, 2015). For the purpose of this study the used value of the capital-output ratio is 2.2. It is calculated as the average gross-capital-formation-to-change-in-real-GDP ratio for the period 1998-2008 (in accordance with the assumption of Harrod and Domar that the average and the marginal productivity of capital are equal). Hence, the actual real size of capital stock **K** can be determined by multiplying the real GDP **Y** by the capital/output ratio **K/Y,** whose value is 2.2:

(3.4) $\mathbf{K = Y * K/Y = Y * 2.2}$

The estimated values of capital stock are shown in Table 3.1.

Table 3.1. Estimated values of capital stock

Year	Real GDP (Y) at prices of 2010, million levs	Capital/output ratio (K/Y)	Capital stock (K) at prices of 2010, million levs
2010	74 771	2.2	164 497
2011	76 203	2.2	167 647
2012	76 227	2.2	167 699
2013	76 884	2.2	169 144
2014	77 906	2.2	171 392
2015	80 724	2.2	177 592

Source: Own calculation on the basis of data from the website of the National Statistical Institute of Bulgaria www.nsi.bg

Two indicators can be used to measure labor input in the production function - the number of employed persons or the number of hours worked in an economy. In this monograph the first indicator is employed.

The potential (optimal) employments of labor is calculated as

(3.5) LPOT = LF * (1 – NRU)

where **LPOT** is the potential (optimal) employments of labor resources, **LF** is the labor force and **NRU** is the natural rate of unemployment.

The natural rate of unemployment is a sum of the rates of structural and frictional unemployment:

(3.6) NRU = SUR + FUR

where **NRU** is the natural rate of unemployment, **SUR** is the structural unemployment rate and **FUR** is the frictional unemployment rate.

As an approximation for the structural unemployment rate **SUR** the long-term unemployment rate **LTUR** is used:

(3.7) SUR = LTUR

The long-term unemployment rate **LTUR** is the percentage share of the long-term unemployed **LTU** in the labor force **LF:**

(3.8) LTUR = (LTU / LF) * 100%

The frictional unemployment rate is calculated as a difference between the rates of outflows and inflows of employees under labor contract:

(3.9) FUR = OREULC – IREULC

where **FUR** is the frictional unemployment rate, **OREULC** is the outflow rate of employees under labor contract and **IREULC** is the inflow rate of employees under labor contract.

The outflow rate of employees under labor contract **OREULC** is the percentage share of the outflow of employees under labor contract **OEULC** in the labor force **LF:**

(3.10) OREULC = (OEULC / LF) * 100

The inflow rate of employees under labor contract **IREULC** is the percentage share of the inflow of employees under labor contract **IEULC** in the labor force **LF:**

(3.11) IREULC = (IEULC / LF) * 100

The natural rate of unemployment **NRU** can be expressed as

(3.12) NRU = LTUR + OREULC – IREULC = (LTE + OEULC – IEULC) / LF *100

The potential (optimal) employment of labor resources **LPOT** can be calculated as

(3.13) LPOT = LF * (1 – LTUR - OREULC + IREULC) = LF – LTE – OEULC + IEULC

The estimated values of the potential employment of labor resources and of the natural rate of unemployment can be seen in Table 3.2.

Table 3.2. Estimation of the potential employment of labor resources

Year	Labor force LF, thousands of people	Long-term unemployment LTUR, %	Outflow rate of employees under labor contract OREULC, %	Inflow rate of employees under labor contract IREULC, %	Natural rate of unemployment NRU, %	Potential employment of labor resources LPOT, thousands of people
2010	3 428	4.75	27.00	26.48	5.27	3 247
2011	3 341	6.30	27.71	28.70	5.32	3 164
2012	3 344	6.78	27.77	28.53	6.02	3 143
2013	3 371	7.43	27.59	28.90	6.12	3 165
2014	3 366	6.93	29.18	30.85	5.26	3 189
2015	3 337	5.60	31.09	32.67	4.02	3 203

Source: Own calculation on the basis of data from the website of the National Statistical Institute of Bulgaria www.nsi.bg

For each year of the period 2010-2015 total factor productivity is calculated as

(3.14) $A_t = Y_t / (K_t^{0.35} * L_t^{0.65})$

where $\mathbf{A_t}$ is total factor productivity in year **t**, $\mathbf{Y_t}$ is GDP in year **t** at prices of 2010 in millions of levs, $\mathbf{K_t}$ is capital stock in year **t** at prices of 2010 in millions of levs and $\mathbf{L_t}$ is the number of employed persons in thousands.

The values of total factor productivity are displayed in Table 3.3.

Table 3.3. Estimates of total factor productivity and Bulgaria's potential output

Year	Total factor productivity A_t	Potential GDP (YPOT), million levs at prices of 2010	Actual GDP (Y), million levs at prices of 2010
2010	6.04	77 457	74 771
2011	6.26	79 481	76 203
2012	6.30	79 713	76 227
2013	6.34	80 751	76 884
2014	6.33	81 388	77 906
2015	6.41	83 656	80 724

Source: *Own calculation on the basis of data from the website of the National Statistical Institute of Bulgaria* www.nsi.bg

In this research for the estimation of Bulgaria's potential outputs is used Equation (3.15), which is a concretization of Equation (3.1):

$$(3.15)\ YPOT = A * (Y * 2.2)^{0.35} * [(LF * (1 - LTUR - OREULC + IREULC)]^{0.65} = A * (Y * 2.2)^{0.35} * (LF - LTE - OEULC + IEULC)^{0.65}$$

The values of the potential and the actual GDP of Bulgaria for the period 2010-2015 are shown in Table 3.3.

Results and inferences from the estimation of Bulgaria's potential GDP and cyclical position

Over the entire period 2010-2015 Bulgaria's output remained below its potential level (see Figure 3.1). The average value of the actual GDP for the period was 77 119 million levs, while the average value of the potential GDP was 80 408 million levs. The stabilities of the dynamics of potential output and actual output were alike (a coefficient of variation of 2.59% for potential GDP and 2.65% for actual GDP).

Figure 3.1. Potential and actual GDP at prices of 2010, million levs

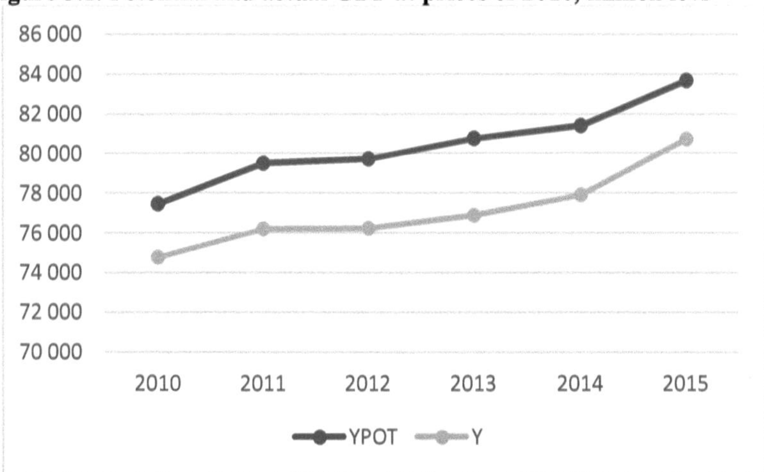

Source: Own calculation on the basis of data from the website of the National Statistical Institute of Bulgaria www.nsi.bg

The growth rates of actual and potential output compared to the previous year were comparable in size (average values of 1.55% и 1.56% respectively for the period 2011-2015). The direction of their movements was different only in 2013-2014 when the growth rate of actual output increased but the growth rate of potential output decreased (see Figure3.2). The growth rates of potential GDP (with a coefficient of variation of 71.00%) were steadier than those of actual GDP (with a coefficient of variation of 86.73%).

Figure 3.2. Rates of growth of potential and actual GDP compared to the previous year, percentage

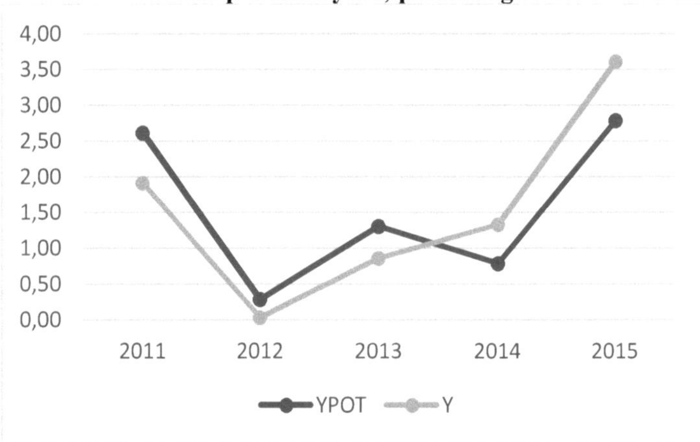

Source: Own calculation on the basis of data from the website of the National Statistical Institute of Bulgaria www.nsi.bg

Figure 3.3. GDP gap (difference between potential and actual output), percentage share of potential GDP

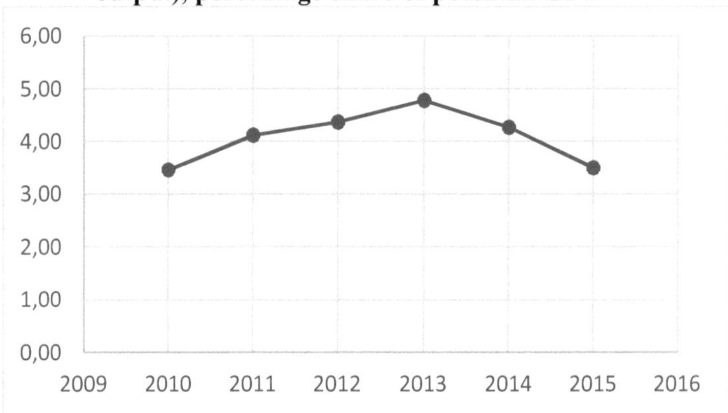

Source: Own calculation on the basis of data from the website of the National Statistical Institute of Bulgaria www.nsi.bg

The difference between potential and actual GDP, measured as a percentage of potential output (the so called GDP gap) increased during 2010-2013 and decreased in 2013-2015 (see Figure 3.3), but remained relatively high for the period 2010-2015 (an average value of 4.09%). The dynamics of the GDP gap was relatively stable (a coefficient of variation of 12.64% for the period 2010-2015).

Figure 3.4. Dynamics of the basic types of unemployment, percentage

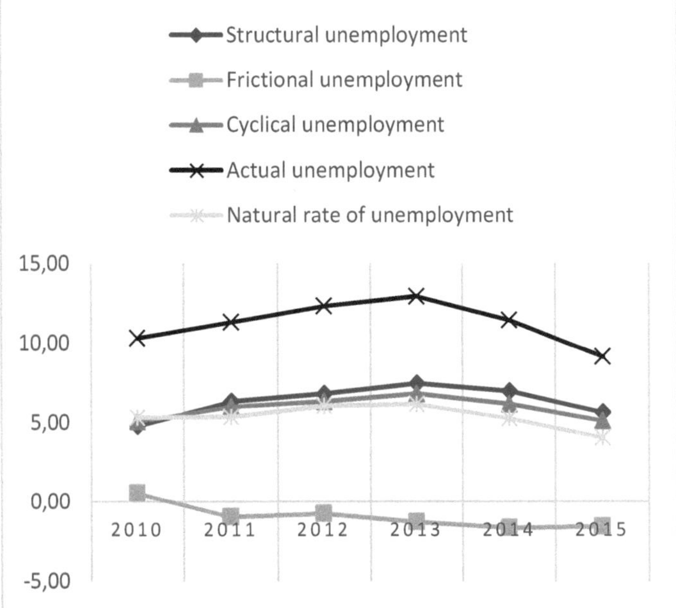

Source: Own calculation on the basis of data from the website of the National Statistical Institute of Bulgaria www.nsi.bg

The dynamics of the basic types of unemployment is interesting (see Figure 3.4). Over the entire period 2010-2015 the actual unemployment rate (an average value of 11.22%) was above the natural rate of unemployment (an average value of 5.33%), while structural and cyclical unemployment had an approximately equal contribution to actual unemployment (average values of 6.30% for structural and 5.88% for cyclical unemployment). The contribution of frictional unemployment to actual unemployment was small (an average of -0.96% for the analyzed period). The movements of the natural rate of unemployment, the actual unemployment rate, the structural unemployment rate and the cyclical unemployment rate were relatively steady (coefficients of variation of 14.10%, 12.20%, 15.52% and 11.82% respectively). However, the dynamics of frictional unemployment was unstable (a coefficient of variation of -83.83%). It may be inferred that a serious problem in the Bulgarian labor market is the existence of high structural unemployment. Increased investment in human capital formation is recommended in order to overcome the differences between the requirements of employers and the qualification of job seekers.

Figure 3.5. Dynamics of capital stock, million levs

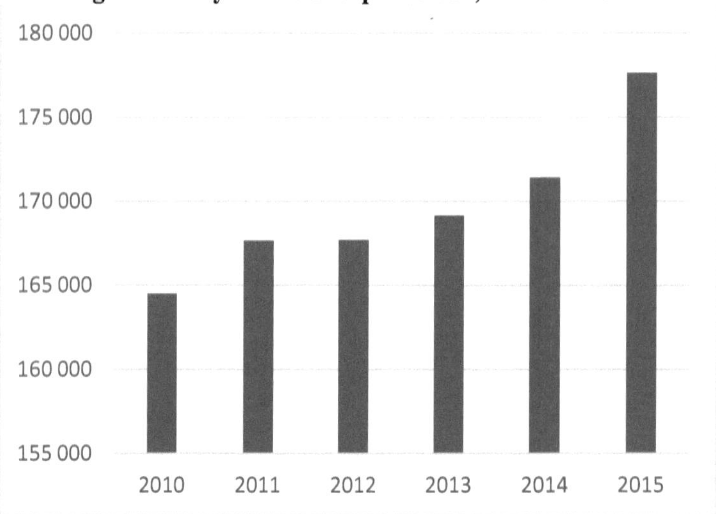

Source: Own calculation on the basis of data from the website of the National Statistical Institute of Bulgaria www.nsi.bg

Capital stock rose in 2010-2015 (see Figure 3.5). The average capital stock for the period of investigation was 169 662 million levs, and its dynamics was stable (a coefficient of variation of 2.65%).

A reason to be optimistic about the future development of the Bulgarian economy is the upward movement of total factor productivity (see Figure 3.6). Total factor productivity is the most important determinant of the long-term economic growth and the standard of living of a nation. Under the conditions of limited quantities of factors of production, the permanent improvement of production efficiency is the only way to continuously improve the welfare of a nation. The dynamics of the total factor productivity reflects the influence of all sources of real GDP growth which are not changes in employment and in physical capital accumulation, such as research and development and the formation of human capital. Total factor productivity increased from 6.04 in 2010 to 6.41 in 2015 and its average for the period 2010-2015 was 6.28 implying that economic efficiency has risen due to improvements in technology and/or organization of production. Total factor productivity is the main contributor to Bulgaria's economic growth under a currency board arrangement (Todorov and Durova, 2016).

Figure 3.6. Dynamics of total factor productivity

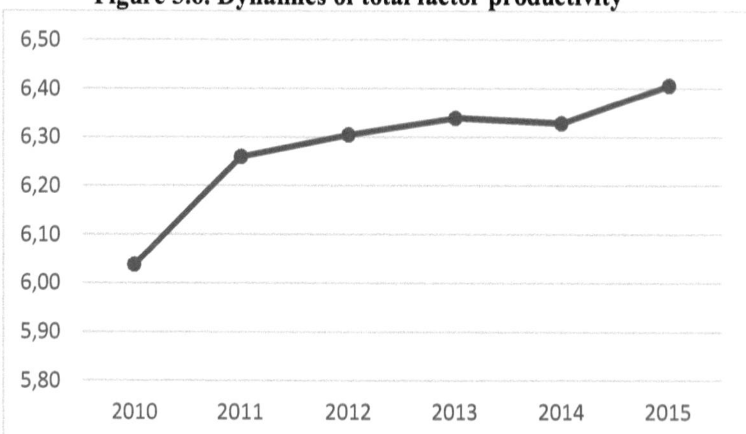

Source: Own calculation on the basis of data from the website of the National Statistical Institute of Bulgaria www.nsi.bg

3.3. The main types of markets and their disequilibria

The labor market

The labor market is in equilibrium when the actual rate of unemployment **ARU** equals the natural rate of unemployment **NRU:**

(3.16) ARU = NRU

The actual rate of unemployment **ARU** is the share of unemployed persons **UP in the** labor force **LF:**

(3.17) ARU = UP / LF

The natural rate of unemployment **NRU** is a sum of the frictional unemployment rate **FUR** and the structural unemployment rate **SUR:**

(3.18) NRU = FUR + SUR

The frictional unemployment rate **FUR** is the share of the difference between the outflow of employees under labor contract **OEULC** and the inflow of employees under labor contract **IEULC** in the labor force **LF:**

(3.19) FUR = (OEULC – IEULC) / LF

The structural unemployment rate **SUR** is the ratio of long-term unemployed persons **LTUP** to the labor force **LF:**

(3.20) SUR = LTUP / LF

If **FUR** and **SUR** are substituted in Equation (3.18) by the right-hand sides of Equations (3.19) and (3.20), then **NRU** can be calculated as

(3.21) NRU = (OEULC – IEULC + LTUP) / LF

Figure 3.7. Actual rate of unemployment and natural unemployment rate in the Bulgaria's labor market for the period 2010-2015

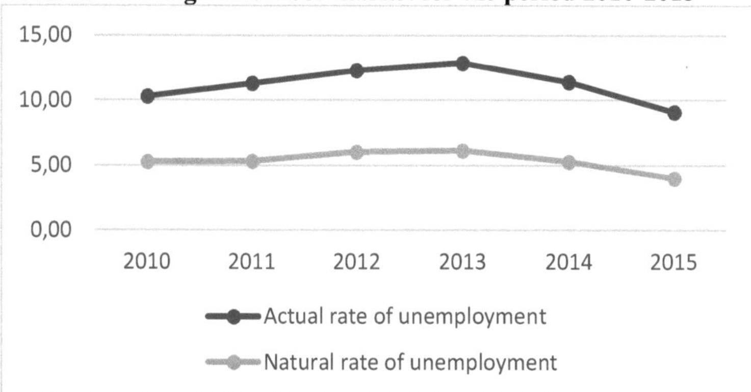

Source: Own calculation on the basis of data from the website of the National Statistical Institute of Bulgaria www.nsi.bg

The labor market equilibrium condition can also be expressed as an equality between the numbers of actually employed persons **AEP** and potentially employed persons **PEP:**

(3.22) AEP = PEP

The number of potentially employed persons **PEP** can be calculated as

(3.23) PEP = LF * (1 – NRU),

where **LF** is the labor force and **NRU** is the natural rate of unemployment.

Figure 3.8. Labor force, actually employed persons and potentially employed persons in Bulgaria's labor market for the period 2010-2015

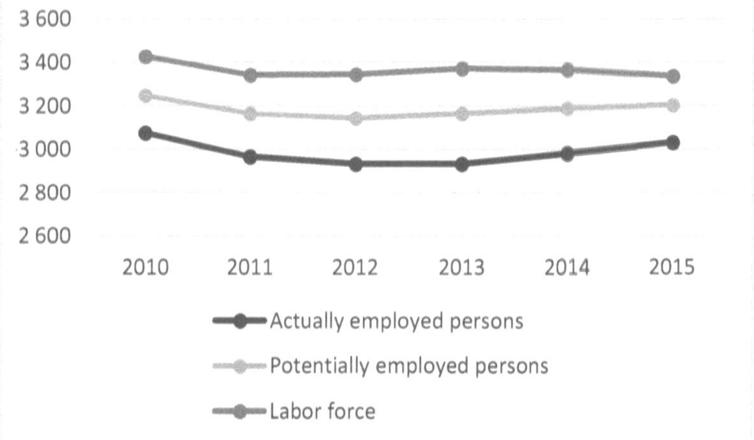

Source: Own calculation on the basis of data from the website of the National Statistical Institute of Bulgaria www.nsi.bg

Bulgaria's labor market was not in equilibrium during 2010-2015. Over the entire period 2010-2015 unemployment was above its natural rate, while employment was below its potential level (see Figures 3.7 and 3.8). Cyclical unemployment was present in 2010-2015, which presumed the implementation of expansive macroeconomic policies.

The goods market

The goods market clearance condition demands that actual national saving **ANS** equal equilibrium national saving **ENS**:

(3.24) ANS = ENS

Actual national saving **ANS** are a sum of private saving **PS** and government saving **GS**:

(3.25) ANS = PS + GS

In an open economy equilibrium national saving **ENS** are a sum of gross capital formation **GCF** and the current account balance **CAB**:

(3.26) ENS = GCF + CAB

Government saving **GS** equals the government budget balance **GBB** and private saving **PS** can be approximated by the change in private deposits (the deposits of non-financial corporations, households and non-profit institutions serving households) **ΔPD**, therefore Equation (3.25) can be modified to

(3.27) ANS = GBB + ΔPD

The goods market clearance condition can be expressed as

(3.28) GBB + ΔPD = GCF + CAB

Figure 3.9. Actual and equilibrium national saving in Bulgaria over the period 2010-2015, million Euros at prices of 2010

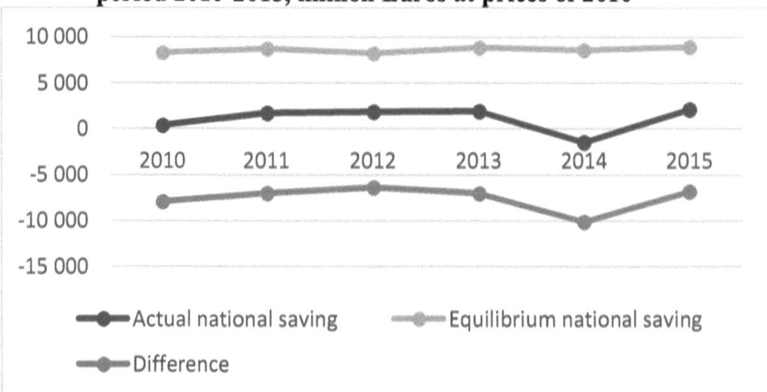

Source: Own calculation on the basis of data from the websites of the Bulgarian National Bank [*www.bnb.bg*](http://www.bnb.bg) *and Eurostat*

Bulgaria's goods market was not in equilibrium over the years 2010-2015 (see Figure 3.9). Over the entire period actual national saving was below its equilibrium level, which agrees with the conclusion that employment and output were below their potential levels.

Figure 3.10. Dynamics of actual national saving, private saving and government saving in Bulgaria for the period 2010-2015, million Euros at prices of 2010

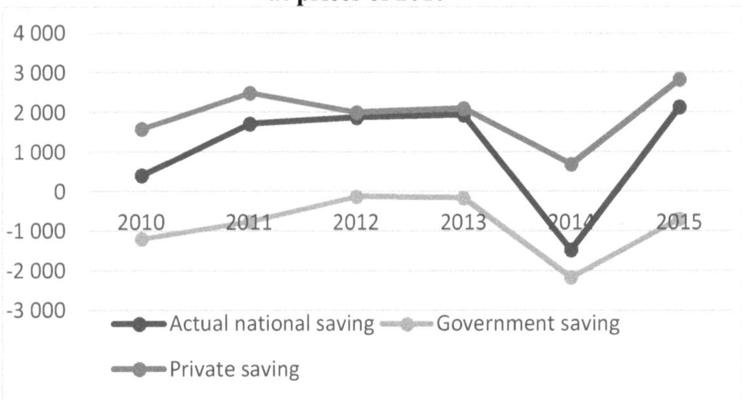

Source: Own calculation on the basis of data from the websites of the Bulgarian National Bank www.bnb.bg and Eurostat

The dynamics of actual national saving depends on the government's fiscal policy and on private saving decisions. Over the entire period 2010-2015 government saving was negative (with an average of -852 million Euros at prices of 2010) but private saving was positive with an average of 1950 million Euros at prices of 2010 (see Figure 3.10). In 2010-2013 and in 2015 positive private saving compensated the government's budget deficits, but in 2014 Bulgaria's actual national saving was negative (–1.5 billion Euros at prices of 2010). The average actual national saving for the period 2010-2015 was positive (1098 million Euros at prices of 2010).

Equilibrium national saving depends on private investment activity and on foreign economic relations.

Figure 3.11. Dynamics of Bulgaria's equilibrium national saving, gross capital formation and current account balance for the period 2010-2015, million Euros at prices of 2010

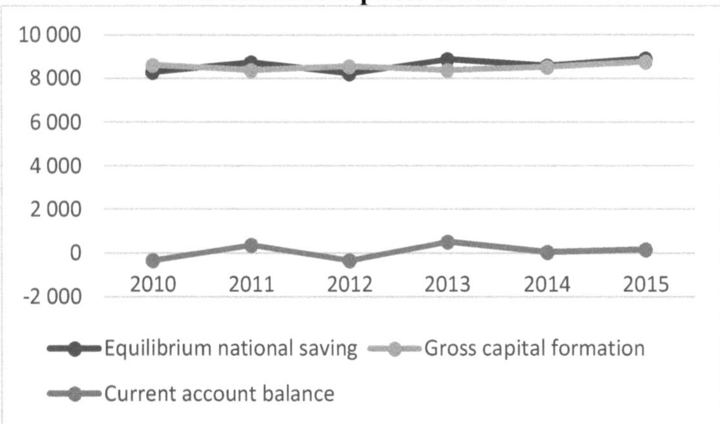

Source: Own calculation on the basis of data from the websites of the Bulgarian National Bank www.bnb.bg *and Eurostat*

Over the entire period 2010-2015 the dynamics of equilibrium national saving (average value of 8600 billion Euros) was determined by domestic investment activity (average gross capital formation of 8536 million Euros), while the impact of foreign sector was insignificant (average current account balance of 64million Euros) (see Figure 11).

Equilibrium national saving **ENS** can be expressed as a linear function of the real interest rate **r** and real GDP **Y**:

(3.29) $\mathbf{ENS_t = a_0 + a_1{*}r_t + a_2{*}Y_t + u_t}$

where $\mathbf{a_0}$ is an intercept term, $\mathbf{a_1}$ and $\mathbf{a_2}$ are regression coefficients and $\mathbf{u_t}$ is an error term.

Equation (3.29) can be estimated via the ordinary lest squares (OLS) method. For the OLS estimation of Equation (3.31) are used quarterly seasonally- and calendar-adjusted Eurostat data on Bulgaria's gross capital formation, current account balance and gross domestic product (in millions of Euros at prices of 2010 г.)

and on the three-month money market interest rate for the period from the first quarter of 2007 to the third quarter of 2015. All data are deflated in order to be transformed from nominal into real.

The Augmented Dickey Fuller (ADF) Unit Root tests indicate that equilibrium national saving and the real interest rate are stationary at the 10% significance level but real GDP is not (see Tables 3.4, 3.5 and 3.6). The ADF test shows that the first differences of real GDP are stationary (see Table 7) at the 10% significance level. Equilibrium national saving and the real interest rate are integrated of order zero I(0), while real GDP is integrated of order 1 I(1). The three time series are not co-integrated because they are integrated of different order. Since the three time series are not co-integrated and an Error Correction Model (ECM) cannot be specified, the process of modeling continues with the first differences of the three variables:

$$\textbf{(3.30)}\ \Delta \mathbf{ENS} = \mathbf{a_0} + \mathbf{a_1} {*} \Delta \mathbf{r} + \mathbf{a_2} {*} \Delta \mathbf{Y} + \mathbf{u_t}$$

Table 3.4. ADF unit root test on equilibrium national saving

Null Hypothesis: ENS has a unit root
Exogenous: Constant
Lag Length: 3 (Automatic - based on SIC, maxlag=8)

		t-Statistic	Prob.*
Augmented Dickey-Fuller test statistic		-3.403984	0.0185
Test critical values:	1% level	-3.661661	
	5% level	-2.960411	
	10% level	-2.619160	

*MacKinnon (1996) one-sided p-values.
Augmented Dickey-Fuller Test Equation
Dependent Variable: D(ENS)
Method: Least Squares
Date: 09/09/16 Time: 13:49
Sample (adjusted): 2008Q1 2015Q3
Included observations: 31 after adjustments

Variable	Coefficient	Std. Error	t-Statistic	Prob.
ENS(-1)	-0.489921	0.143926	-3.403984	0.0022
D(ENS(-1))	-0.468874	0.138414	-3.387462	0.0023
D(ENS(-2))	-0.716840	0.089481	-8.011103	0.0000
D(ENS(-3))	-0.736396	0.101195	-7.276970	0.0000
C	1116.405	285.2579	3.913669	0.0006
R-squared	0.916091	Mean dependent var		88.03950
Adjusted R-squared	0.903182	S.D. dependent var		1005.236
S.E. of regression	312.7858	Akaike info criterion		14.47560
Sum squared resid	2543710.	Schwarz criterion		14.70689
Log likelihood	-219.3719	Hannan-Quinn criter.		14.55100
F-statistic	70.96463	Durbin-Watson stat		2.352058
Prob(F-statistic)	0.000000			

Source: Own calculations on the basis of Eurostat data

Table 3.5. ADF unit root test on the real interest rate

Null Hypothesis: R has a unit root
Exogenous: Constant, Linear Trend
Lag Length: 1 (Automatic - based on SIC, maxlag=8)

		t-Statistic	Prob.*
Augmented Dickey-Fuller test statistic		-3.376330	0.0720
Test critical values:	1% level	-4.262735	
	5% level	-3.552973	
	10% level	-3.209642	

*MacKinnon (1996) one-sided p-values.

Augmented Dickey-Fuller Test Equation
Dependent Variable: D(R)
Method: Least Squares
Date: 09/09/16 Time: 14:01
Sample (adjusted): 2007Q3 2015Q3
Included observations: 33 after adjustments

Variable	Coefficient	Std. Error	t-Statistic	Prob.
R(-1)	-0.254830	0.075476	-3.376330	0.0021
D(R(-1))	0.482781	0.135380	3.566104	0.0013
C	1.963633	0.608217	3.228509	0.0031
@TREND(2007Q1)	-0.062906	0.019175	-3.280658	0.0027

R-squared	0.475052	Mean dependent var	-0.142491
Adjusted R-squared	0.420747	S.D. dependent var	0.447348
S.E. of regression	0.340470	Akaike info criterion	0.796235
Sum squared resid	3.361683	Schwarz criterion	0.977630
Log likelihood	-9.137883	Hannan-Quinn criter.	0.857269
F-statistic	8.747857	Durbin-Watson stat	2.257674
Prob(F-statistic)	0.000275		

Source: Own calculations on the basis of Eurostat data

Table 3.6. ADF unit root test on real GDP

Null Hypothesis: Y has a unit root
Exogenous: Constant, Linear Trend
Lag Length: 8 (Automatic - based on SIC, maxlag=8)

		t-Statistic	Prob.*
Augmented Dickey-Fuller test statistic		-0.605115	0.9700
Test critical values:	1% level	-4.356068	
	5% level	-3.595026	
	10% level	-3.233456	

*MacKinnon (1996) one-sided p-values.
Augmented Dickey-Fuller Test Equation
Dependent Variable: D(Y)
Method: Least Squares
Date: 09/09/16 Time: 14:20
Sample (adjusted): 2009Q2 2015Q3
Included observations: 26 after adjustments

Variable	Coefficient	Std. Error	t-Statistic	Prob.
Y(-1)	-0.206967	0.342030	-0.605115	0.5541
D(Y(-1))	-0.727656	0.287004	-2.535354	0.0229
D(Y(-2))	-0.657918	0.242516	-2.712883	0.0160
D(Y(-3))	-0.584071	0.203578	-2.869031	0.0117
D(Y(-4))	0.244829	0.171892	1.424320	0.1748
D(Y(-5))	-0.219559	0.186340	-1.178273	0.2570
D(Y(-6))	-0.336505	0.169369	-1.986812	0.0655
D(Y(-7))	-0.458441	0.151866	-3.018710	0.0086
D(Y(-8))	-0.337535	0.144272	-2.339575	0.0336
C	1663.007	3173.665	0.524002	0.6079
@TREND(2007Q1)	18.19309	6.823411	2.666275	0.0176

R-squared	0.997351	Mean dependent var	120.9020
Adjusted R-squared	0.995585	S.D. dependent var	1541.483
S.E. of regression	102.4251	Akaike info criterion	12.39225
Sum squared resid	157363.4	Schwarz criterion	12.92452
Log likelihood	-150.0992	Hannan-Quinn criter.	12.54552
F-statistic	564.7457	Durbin-Watson stat	1.906247
Prob(F-statistic)	0.000000		

Source: Own calculations on the basis of Eurostat data

Table 3.7. ADF unit root test on the first differences of real GDP

Null Hypothesis: D(Y) has a unit root
Exogenous: Constant, Linear Trend
Lag Length: 7 (Automatic - based on SIC, maxlag=8)

		t-Statistic	Prob.*
Augmented Dickey-Fuller test statistic		-5.299310	0.0012
Test critical values:	1% level	-4.356068	
	5% level	-3.595026	
	10% level	-3.233456	

*MacKinnon (1996) one-sided p-values.
Augmented Dickey-Fuller Test Equation
Dependent Variable: D(Y,2)
Method: Least Squares
Date: 09/09/16 Time: 14:38
Sample (adjusted): 2009Q2 2015Q3
Included observations: 26 after adjustments

Variable	Coefficient	Std. Error	t-Statistic	Prob.
D(Y(-1))	-4.643720	0.876288	-5.299310	0.0001
D(Y(-1),2)	2.786251	0.720789	3.865557	0.0014
D(Y(-2),2)	2.035973	0.571243	3.564111	0.0026
D(Y(-3),2)	1.387080	0.444338	3.121676	0.0066
D(Y(-4),2)	1.590198	0.344113	4.621148	0.0003
D(Y(-5),2)	1.281036	0.286760	4.467272	0.0004
D(Y(-6),2)	0.870674	0.219101	3.973841	0.0011
D(Y(-7),2)	0.360677	0.136328	2.645654	0.0176
C	-256.6631	87.64684	-2.928378	0.0098
@TREND(2007Q1)	14.97021	4.179863	3.581506	0.0025

R-squared	0.998957	Mean dependent var	152.1089
Adjusted R-squared	0.998370	S.D. dependent var	2486.059
S.E. of regression	100.3758	Akaike info criterion	12.33944
Sum squared resid	161204.8	Schwarz criterion	12.82333
Log likelihood	-150.4127	Hannan-Quinn criter.	12.47878
F-statistic	1702.194	Durbin-Watson stat	1.974016
Prob(F-statistic)	0.000000		

Source: Own calculations on the basis of Eurostat data

The results from the OLS-estimation of Equation (3.30) are displayed in Table 3.8.

Table 3.8. OLS-estimates of the parameters of Equation (3.30)

Dependent Variable: D(ENS,1)
Method: Least Squares
Date: 09/09/16 Time: 14:49
Sample (adjusted): 2007Q2 2015Q3
Included observations: 34 after adjustments

Variable	Coefficient	Std. Error	t-Statistic	Prob.
C	-17.88175	136.4773	-0.131024	0.8966
D(R,1)	-524.2865	299.4413	-1.750882	0.0899
D(Y,1)	0.431693	0.087952	4.908288	0.0000

R-squared	0.443528	Mean dependent var	90.05183
Adjusted R-squared	0.407626	S.D. dependent var	987.9449
S.E. of regression	760.3800	Akaike info criterion	16.18961
Sum squared resid	17923511	Schwarz criterion	16.32429
Log likelihood	-272.2234	Hannan-Quinn criter.	16.23554
F-statistic	12.35403	Durbin-Watson stat	2.733361
Prob(F-statistic)	0.000113		

Source: Own calculations on the basis of Eurostat data

At the 5% level the intercept and the real interest rate are not significant but real GDP is. At the 10% level the real interest rate also becomes significant. The estimated value of $\mathbf{a_1}$ (-524.2865) means that a 1% change in the three-month money interest rate will lead to a national saving change of 524.2865 million Euros in the opposite direction, provided that GDP is held constant. The estimated value of $\mathbf{a_2}$ (0.431693) indicates that a one-million-Euro change in GDP will lead to a 0.43-million-Euro change in national saving in the same direction, if the three-month money interest rate remains unchanged.

The coefficient of determination ($R^2 = 0.443528$) shows that 44.35% of changes in national saving during the period of investigation can be explained by changes in GDP and the interest rate. The probability of the F-statistic (0.000113) indicates that at the 5% level of significance the alternative hypothesis for the adequacy of the regression model is accepted. The acceptance of the alternative hypothesis does not mean that the model specification is the best possible but only that the regression model adequately reflects the relationship between dependent variable and independent variables.

The residual heteroscedasticity test (ARCH) confirms the null hypothesis for the absence of heteroscedasticity at the 5% level of significance (see Table 3.9). The residual normality test (Jarque-Bera) confirms the null hypothesis for the presence of normal distribution of residuals at the 5% level of significance (see Figure 3.12). The value of 2.733361of the Durbin-Watson statistic presumes the existence of serial correlation (autocorrelation) of residuals. At the 5% level of significance the serial correlation LM test confirms the alternative hypothesis that residuals are serially correlated (see Table 3.10). The serial correlation of residuals is not unusual for time-series data. In the presence of serial correlation OLS estimates and based on them forecasts are inefficient but still unbiased and consistent. Since the regression model will not be used for forecasting, the serial correlation has not been removed from the model.

Table 3.9. Heteroscedasticity test (ARCH) on the residuals of Equation (3.29)

Heteroscedasticity Test: ARCH

F-statistic	1.941651	Prob. F(1,31)	0.1734
Obs*R-squared	1.945090	Prob. Chi-Square(1)	0.1631

Test Equation:
Dependent Variable: RESID^2
Method: Least Squares
Date: 09/09/16 Time: 15:12
Sample (adjusted): 2007Q3 2015Q3
Included observations: 33 after adjustments

Variable	Coefficient	Std. Error	t-Statistic	Prob.
C	665373.8	143140.4	4.648399	0.0001
RESID^2 (-1)	-0.241707	0.173461	-1.393431	0.1734

R-squared	0.058942	Mean dependent var	539658.4
Adjusted R-squared	0.028585	S.D. dependent var	647708.5
S.E. of regression	638383.9	Akaike info criterion	29.62996
Sum squared resid	1.26E+13	Schwarz criterion	29.72066
Log likelihood	-486.8943	Hannan-Quinn criter.	29.66048
F-statistic	1.941651	Durbin-Watson stat	2.214889
Prob(F-statistic)	0.173400		

Source: Own calculations on the basis of Eurostat data

Figure 3.12. Histogram of the residuals of Equation (3.29)

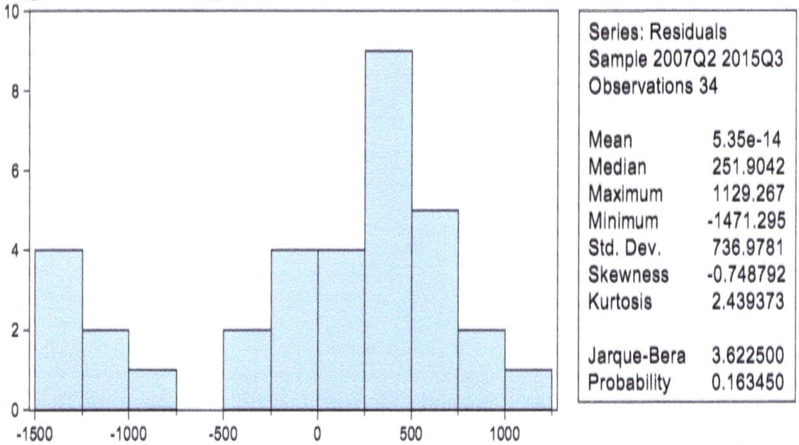

Source: Own calculations on the basis of Eurostat data

Table 3.10. Serial correlation LM test on the residuals of Equation (3.29)

Breusch-Godfrey Serial Correlation LM Test:

F-statistic	10.92799	Prob. F(2,29)	0.0003
Obs*R-squared	14.61191	Prob. Chi-Square(2)	0.0007

Test Equation:
Dependent Variable: RESID
Method: Least Squares
Date: 09/09/16 Time: 15:28
Sample: 2007Q2 2015Q3
Included observations: 34
Presample missing value lagged residuals set to zero.

Variable	Coefficient	Std. Error	t-Statistic	Prob.
C	-28.01203	107.0088	-0.261773	0.7953
D(R,1)	296.9699	250.1303	1.187261	0.2448
D(Y,1)	0.380497	0.113159	3.362487	0.0022
RESID(-1)	-1.099789	0.235833	-4.663431	0.0001
RESID(-2)	-0.008930	0.171851	-0.051965	0.9589

R-squared	0.429762	Mean dependent var	5.35E-14
Adjusted R-squared	0.351109	S.D. dependent var	736.9781
S.E. of regression	593.6638	Akaike info criterion	15.74556
Sum squared resid	10220664	Schwarz criterion	15.97002
Log likelihood	-262.6745	Hannan-Quinn criter.	15.82211
F-statistic	5.463993	Durbin-Watson stat	2.029708
Prob(F-statistic)	0.002099		

Source: Own calculations on the basis of Eurostat data

Ramsey's Regression Specification Error Test (RESET) alludes to the presence of unsolved specification problems in Equation 3.29 such as non-linearity or omitted variables (see Table 3.11). The Granger Causality Test confirms the alternative hypothesis for the presence of a causal relationship at the 5% level of significance in the following directions (see Table 3.12):

- From the real interest rate to national saving;
- From real GDP to national saving;
- From national saving to real GDP.

The Granger Causality Test confirms the null hypothesis for the absence of a causal relationship at the 5% level of significance in the following directions (see Table 3.12):

- From national saving to the real interest rate;
- From real GDP to the real interest rate;
- From the real interest rate to real GDP.

Table 3.11. Regression Specification Error Test on Equation (3.29)

Ramsey RESET Test
Equation: EQ01
Specification: D(ENS,1) C D(R,1) D(Y,1)
Omitted Variables: Squares of fitted values

	Value	df	Probability
t-statistic	3.245758	30	0.0029
F-statistic	10.53495	(1, 30)	0.0029
Likelihood ratio	10.23288	1	0.0014

F-test summary:

	Sum of Sq.	df	Mean Squares
Test SSR	4658283.	1	4658283.
Restricted SSR	17923511	31	578177.8
Unrestricted SSR	13265228	30	442174.3
Unrestricted SSR	13265228	30	442174.3

LR test summary:

	Value	df
Restricted LogL	-272.2234	31
Unrestricted LogL	-267.1069	30

Unrestricted Test Equation:
Dependent Variable: D(ENS,1)
Method: Least Squares
Date: 09/09/16 Time: 15:42
Sample: 2007Q2 2015Q3
Included observations: 34

Variable	Coefficient	Std. Error	t-Statistic	Prob.
C	-509.9514	192.9467	-2.642965	0.0129
D(R,1)	-483.2556	262.1701	-1.843290	0.0752
D(Y,1)	0.549217	0.085012	6.460497	0.0000
FITTED^2	0.001134	0.000349	3.245758	0.0029

R-squared	0.588154	Mean dependent var	90.05183
Adjusted R-squared	0.546969	S.D. dependent var	987.9449
S.E. of regression	664.9619	Akaike info criterion	15.94747
Sum squared resid	13265228	Schwarz criterion	16.12704
Log likelihood	-267.1069	Hannan-Quinn criter.	16.00871
F-statistic	14.28089	Durbin-Watson stat	2.799710
Prob(F-statistic)	0.000006		

Source: Own calculations on the basis of Eurostat data

Table 3.12. Granger Causality Test on Equation (3.29)

Pairwise Granger Causality Tests
Date: 09/09/16 Time: 15:56
Sample: 2007Q1 2015Q3
Lags: 2

Null Hypothesis:	Obs	F-Statistic	Prob.
R does not Granger Cause ENS	33	10.8230	0.0003
ENS does not Granger Cause R		2.84882	0.0748
Y does not Granger Cause ENS	33	25.8671	4.E-07
ENS does not Granger Cause Y		22.3883	2.E-06
Y does not Granger Cause R	33	1.30172	0.2880
R does not Granger Cause Y		0.68546	0.5121

Source: Own calculations on the basis of Eurostat data

If the regression coefficients $\mathbf{a_0}$, $\mathbf{a_1}$ and $\mathbf{a_2}$ are substituted in Equation (3.30) by their OLS-estimates, Equation (3.30) becomes

(3.31) $\mathbf{\Delta ENS = -17.88 - 524.29 * \Delta r + 0.43 * \Delta Y + u_t}$

The equilibrium value of real GDP for the goods market in moment t $\mathbf{GMEY_t}$ can be calculated by transforming Equation (3.31) to

(3.32) $\mathbf{GMEY_t = (17.88 + \Delta ENS + 0.43 * Y_{t-1} + 524.29 * \Delta r) / 0.43}$

Equation (3.32) is the **IS** curve equation.

Figure 3.13. Actual and equilibrium values of real GDP for the goods market over the period 2007Q2 - 2015Q3, million Euros at prices of 2010

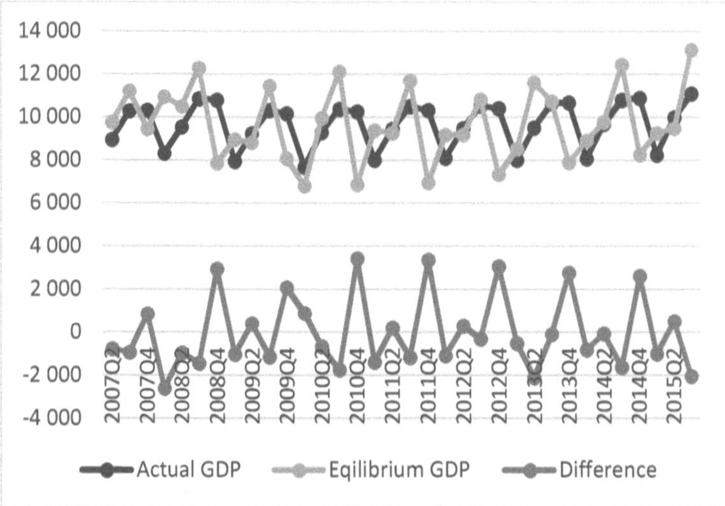

Source: Own calculations on the basis of Eurostat data

In Figure 3.13 are displayed the values of actual real GDP, the equilibrium values of real GDP for the goods market (calculated by Equation 3.32) and their differences for the period 2007Q2- 2015Q3. It can be concluded that the goods market was near its equilibrium level in both periods 2010-2015 and 2007-2015.

The money market

The money market equilibrium condition demands that the real demand for money **MD/P** be equal to the real money supply **MS/P**:

(3.33) MD/P = MS/P

where **MD** is the nominal demand for money, **MS** is the nominal money supply, and **P** is a price index (the GDP deflator).

The real demand for money **MD/P** can be presented as a linear function of the real interest rate **r** and real GDP **Y**:

(3.34) $\mathbf{MD/P = b_0 + b_1 * r + b_2 * Y + u}$

where $\mathbf{b_0}$, $\mathbf{b_1}$ and $\mathbf{b_2}$ are regression coefficients and **u** is an error term.

The money market equilibrium condition can be expressed as

(3.35) $\mathbf{MD/P = MS/P = b_0 + b_1 * r + b_2 * Y + u}$

Equation (3.34) can be estimated by the OLS method to obtain the values of the regression coefficients $\mathbf{b_0}$, $\mathbf{b_1}$ and $\mathbf{b_2}$. Under the OLS procedure are used nominal quarterly data on the monetary aggregate M3, GDP and the three-month money market interest rate, which are divided by the GDP deflator for the respective quarter.

It is already known from Section 2.2 that the real interest rate is integrated of order zero I(0), while real GDP is integrated of order 1 I(1). The monetary aggregate M3 is also integrated of order I(1) (see Tables 3.12 and 3.13).

Table 3.13. ADF unit root test on the monetary aggregate M3

Null Hypothesis: M3 has a unit root
Exogenous: Constant, Linear Trend
Lag Length: 0 (Automatic - based on SIC, maxlag=10)

		t-Statistic	Prob.*
Augmented Dickey-Fuller test statistic		-2.763647	0.2159
Test critical values:	1% level	-4.107947	
	5% level	-3.481595	
	10% level	-3.168695	

*MacKinnon (1996) one-sided p-values.

Augmented Dickey-Fuller Test Equation
Dependent Variable: D(M3)
Method: Least Squares
Date: 09/09/16 Time: 19:41
Sample (adjusted): 1999Q4 2015Q3
Included observations: 64 after adjustments

Variable	Coefficient	Std. Error	t-Statistic	Prob.
M3(-1)	-0.222253	0.080420	-2.763647	0.0075
C	1556.289	442.9392	3.513550	0.0008
@TREND(1999Q3)	99.43456	36.25035	2.742996	0.0080

R-squared	0.111278	Mean dependent var	428.8706
Adjusted R-squared	0.082139	S.D. dependent var	705.9149
S.E. of regression	676.3021	Akaike info criterion	15.91690
Sum squared resid	27900456	Schwarz criterion	16.01810
Log likelihood	-506.3407	Hannan-Quinn criter.	15.95676
F-statistic	3.818938	Durbin-Watson stat	1.943395
Prob(F-statistic)	0.027376		

Source: Own calculations on the basis of Eurostat data

The three time series are not co-integrated because they are integrated of different order. Since the three time series are not co-integrated and an Error Correction Model (ECM) cannot be specified, the process of modeling continues with the first differences of the three variables:

$$\textbf{(3.36)}\ \Delta(M3/P) = b_0 + b_1{*}\Delta r + b_2{*}\Delta Y + u$$

The results from the OLS-estimation of Equation (3.36) are displayed in Table 3.14.

Table 3.14. ADF unit root test on the first differences of the monetary aggregate M3

Null Hypothesis: D(M3) has a unit root
Exogenous: Constant, Linear Trend
Lag Length: 0 (Automatic - based on SIC, maxlag=10)

		t-Statistic	Prob.*
Augmented Dickey-Fuller test statistic		-8.380004	0.0000
Test critical values:	1% level	-4.110440	
	5% level	-3.482763	
	10% level	-3.169372	

*MacKinnon (1996) one-sided p-values.
Augmented Dickey-Fuller Test Equation
Dependent Variable: D(M3,2)
Method: Least Squares
Date: 09/09/16 Time: 19:50
Sample (adjusted): 2000Q1 2015Q3
Included observations: 63 after adjustments

Variable	Coefficient	Std. Error	t-Statistic	Prob.
D(M3(-1))	-1.102006	0.131504	-8.380004	0.0000
C	488.9936	197.5865	2.474833	0.0162
@TREND(1999Q3)	-0.451651	4.988297	-0.090542	0.9282

R-squared	0.539572	Mean dependent var	22.14552
Adjusted R-squared	0.524225	S.D. dependent var	1042.675
S.E. of regression	719.2002	Akaike info criterion	16.04060
Sum squared resid	31034938	Schwarz criterion	16.14266
Log likelihood	-502.2790	Hannan-Quinn criter.	16.08074
F-statistic	35.15682	Durbin-Watson stat	1.984274
Prob(F-statistic)	0.000000		

Source: Own calculations on the basis of Eurostat data

Table 3.15: OLS-estimates of the parameters of Equation (3.36)
Dependent Variable: D(M3,1)
Method: Least Squares
Date: 09/09/16 Time: 20:03
Sample (adjusted): 1999Q4 2015Q3
Included observations: 64 after adjustments

Variable	Coefficient	Std. Error	t-Statistic	Prob.
C	426.8034	87.19232	4.894966	0.0000
D(R,1)	58.52849	111.8706	0.523180	0.6027
D(Y,1)	0.148536	0.065668	2.261913	0.0273

R-squared	0.092959	Mean dependent var	428.8706
Adjusted R-squared	0.063220	S.D. dependent var	705.9149
S.E. of regression	683.2366	Akaike info criterion	15.93730
Sum squared resid	28475549	Schwarz criterion	16.03850
Log likelihood	-506.9936	Hannan-Quinn criter.	15.97717
F-statistic	3.125832	Durbin-Watson stat	2.232449
Prob(F-statistic)	0.051006		

Source: Own calculations on the basis of Eurostat data

At the 5% level the intercept and the regression coefficient before real GDP are statistically significant. The estimated value of the intercept $\mathbf{b_0}$ (426.8034) indicates that in the hypothetical situation of a zero real GDP and a zero real interest rate Bulgaria would have a real equilibrium demand for money of 426.80 million Euros at prices of 2010. Such a situation could be explained by the need for a monetary exchange of goods and services even at zero values of real GDP and the real interest rate. The estimated value of $\mathbf{b_2}$ (0.148536) suggests that a one-million shift in GDP will change the equilibrium demand for money by 0.15 million Euros in the same direction provided that the three-month money market interest rate remains unchanged.

The coefficient of determination (R^2 = 0.092959) shows that 9.3% of the variations in the equilibrium demand for money during the period of investigation can be explained by changes in GDP and the interest rate. The probability of the F-statistic (0.051006) indicates that at the 10% level of significance the alternative hypothesis for the adequacy of the regression model is accepted. The acceptance of the alternative hypothesis does not mean that the model specification is the best possible but only that the regression model adequately reflects the relationship between dependent variable and independent variables.

The residual heteroscedasticity test (Breusch-Pagan-Godfrey) confirms the null hypothesis for the absence of heteroscedasticity at the 5% level of significance (see Table 3.15).

Table 3.16. Residual heteroscedasticity test (Breusch-Pagan-Godfrey) on Equation 3.36

Heteroscedasticity Test: Breusch-Pagan-Godfrey

F-statistic	0.512521	Prob. F(2,61)	0.6015
Obs*R-squared	1.057680	Prob. Chi-Square(2)	0.5893
Scaled explained SS	0.717245	Prob. Chi-Square(2)	0.6986

Test Equation:
Dependent Variable: RESID^2
Method: Least Squares
Date: 09/11/16 Time: 10:53
Sample: 1999Q4 2015Q3
Included observations: 64

Variable	Coefficient	Std. Error	t-Statistic	Prob.
C	459054.6	70473.73	6.513839	0.0000
D(R,1)	82639.45	90420.08	0.913950	0.3643
D(Y,1)	-33.54676	53.07682	-0.632042	0.5297

R-squared	0.016526	Mean dependent var	444930.4
Adjusted R-squared	-0.015719	S.D. dependent var	547940.6
S.E. of regression	552230.2	Akaike info criterion	29.32706
Sum squared resid	1.86E+13	Schwarz criterion	29.42826
Log likelihood	-935.4659	Hannan-Quinn criter.	29.36693
F-statistic	0.512521	Durbin-Watson stat	1.761145
Prob(F-statistic)	0.601540		

Source: Own calculations on the basis of Eurostat data

The residual normality test (Jarque-Bera) confirms the null hypothesis for the presence of normal distribution of residuals at the 5% level of significance (see Figure 3.14).

Figure 3.14. Histogram of the residuals of Equation (3.36)

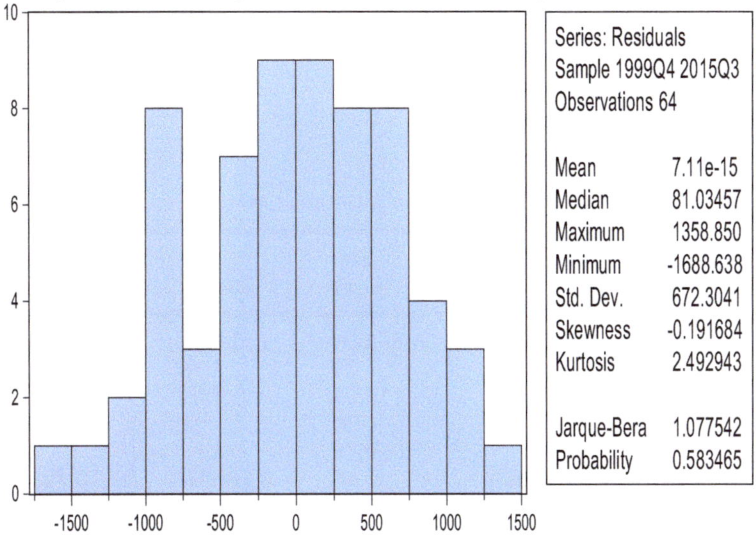

Source: Own calculations on the basis of Eurostat data

The value of 2.232449 of the Durbin-Watson statistic presumes the lack of serial correlation (autocorrelation) of residuals. At the 5% level of significance the serial correlation LM test confirms the null hypothesis that residuals are not serially correlated (see Table 3.16).

Table 3.17. Residual Serial Correlation LM Test (Breusch-Pagan-Godfrey) on Equation 3.36

Breusch-Godfrey Serial Correlation LM Test:

F-statistic	0.722980	Prob. F(2,59)	0.4896
Obs*R-squared	1.530977	Prob. Chi-Square(2)	0.4651

Test Equation:
Dependent Variable: RESID
Method: Least Squares
Date: 09/11/16 Time: 11:08
Sample: 1999Q4 2015Q3
Included observations: 64
Presample missing value lagged residuals set to zero.

Variable	Coefficient	Std. Error	t-Statistic	Prob.
C	1.441351	87.63479	0.016447	0.9869
D(R,1)	17.73776	113.9170	0.155708	0.8768
D(Y,1)	-0.017990	0.067646	-0.265948	0.7912
RESID(-1)	-0.155307	0.135023	-1.150220	0.2547
RESID(-2)	-0.066343	0.136732	-0.485205	0.6293

R-squared	0.023922	Mean dependent var	7.11E-15
Adjusted R-squared	-0.042253	S.D. dependent var	672.3041
S.E. of regression	686.3607	Akaike info criterion	15.97559
Sum squared resid	27794370	Schwarz criterion	16.14425
Log likelihood	-506.2188	Hannan-Quinn criter.	16.04203
F-statistic	0.361490	Durbin-Watson stat	1.976567
Prob(F-statistic)	0.835023		

Source: Own calculations on the basis of Eurostat data

Ramsey's Regression Specification Error Test (RESET) confirms the null hypothesis for the absence of errors in the specification of the regression model (see Table 3.18).

Table 3.18. Residual Ramsey's Regression Specification Error Test (RESET) on Equation 3.36

Ramsey RESET Test
Equation: EQ01
Specification: D(M3,1) C D(R,1) D(Y,1)
Omitted Variables: Squares of fitted values

	Value	df	Probability
t-statistic	0.273036	60	0.7858
F-statistic	0.074548	(1, 60)	0.7858
Likelihood ratio	0.079469	1	0.7780

F-test summary:

	Sum of Sq.	df	Mean Squares
Test SSR	35336.21	1	35336.21
Restricted SSR	28475549	61	466812.3
Unrestricted SSR	28440212	60	474003.5
Unrestricted SSR	28440212	60	474003.5

LR test summary:

	Value	df
Restricted LogL	-506.9936	61
Unrestricted LogL	-506.9539	60

Unrestricted Test Equation:
Dependent Variable: D(M3,1)
Method: Least Squares
Date: 09/11/16 Time: 11:20
Sample: 1999Q4 2015Q3

Included observations: 64

Variable	Coefficient	Std. Error	t-Statistic	Prob.
C	281.8971	537.9469	0.524024	0.6022
D(R,1)	31.59316	149.7996	0.210903	0.8337
D(Y,1)	0.084374	0.244133	0.345608	0.7308
FITTED^2	0.000634	0.002323	0.273036	0.7858

R-squared	0.094085	Mean dependent var	428.8706
Adjusted R-squared	0.048789	S.D. dependent var	705.9149
S.E. of regression	688.4791	Akaike info criterion	15.96731
Sum squared resid	28440212	Schwarz criterion	16.10224
Log likelihood	-506.9539	Hannan-Quinn criter.	16.02046
F-statistic	2.077122	Durbin-Watson stat	2.214152
Prob(F-statistic)	0.112723		

Source: Own calculations on the basis of Eurostat data

The Granger Causality Test (see Table 3.19) confirms the alternative hypothesis for the presence of a causal relationship at the 5% level of significance in the following directions:

- From real GDP to the equilibrium demand for money;
- From the equilibrium demand for money to real GDP;
- From the real interest rate to real GDP.

The Granger Causality Test (see Table 3.19) confirms the null hypothesis for the absence of a causal relationship at the 5% level of significance in the following directions:

- From the real interest rate to the equilibrium demand for money;

- From the equilibrium demand for money to the real interest rate;
- From real GDP to the real interest rate.

Table 3.19. Granger Causality Test on Equation (3.36)

Pairwise Granger Causality Tests
Date: 09/11/16 Time: 11:24
Sample: 1999Q3 2015Q3
Lags: 2

Null Hypothesis:	Obs	F-Statistic	Prob.
R does not Granger Cause M3	63	2.50958	0.0901
M3 does not Granger Cause R		0.59526	0.5548
Y does not Granger Cause M3	63	3.31237	0.0434
M3 does not Granger Cause Y		30.5957	8.E-10
Y does not Granger Cause R	63	0.45843	0.6345
R does not Granger Cause Y		5.95006	0.0045

Source: Own calculations on the basis of Eurostat data

$$(3.37)\ \Delta(M3/P) = b_0 + b_1*\Delta r + b_2*\Delta Y + u$$

If the regression coefficients b_0, b_1 and b_2 are substituted in Equation (3.36) by their OLS-estimates, Equation (3.36) becomes

$$(3.38)\ \Delta(M3/P) = 429.80 + 58.53*\Delta r + 0.15*\Delta Y + u_t$$

The equilibrium value of real GDP for the goods market in moment t $MMEY_t$ can be calculated by transforming Equation (3.38) to

$$(3.39)\ MMEY_t = (\Delta(M3/P) - 429.80 - 58.53*\Delta r + 0.15*Y_{t-1}) / 0.15$$

Equation (3.39) is the **LM** curve equation.

In Figure 15 are shown the values of actual real GDP, the equilibrium values of real GDP for the money market (calculated by Equation 3.39) and their differences for the period 1999Q4 - 2015Q3. It can be inferred that the money market was much below its equilibrium level in both periods 2010-2015 and 1999-2015. The huge imbalances in Bulgaria's money market can be attributed to the bad condition of the Bulgarian economy (weak growth accompanied by deflationary trends) and to the lack of autonomous monetary policy in Bulgaria under a currency board arrangement.

Figure 3.15. Actual and equilibrium values of real GDP for the money market over the period 1999Q4 - 2015Q3, million Euros at prices of 2010

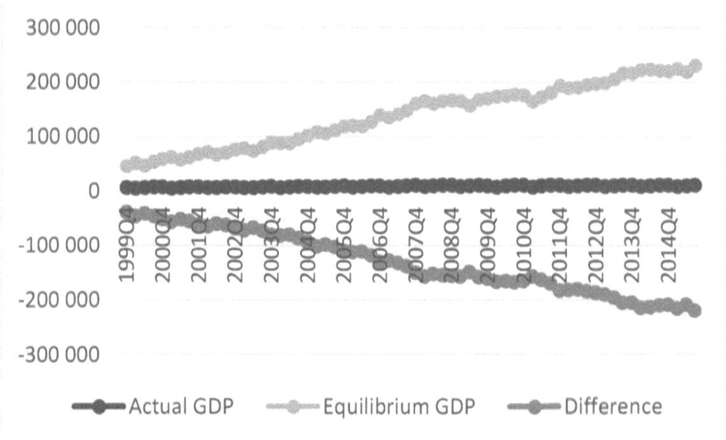

Source: Own calculations on the basis of Eurostat data

https://doi.org/10.2478/9783110619218-005

CONCLUSIONS

Structural Funds are not spent on projects defined at European level. The choice of projects and their management are the sole responsibility of national and regional authorities. These projects are co-financed by national and EU funds. The principle of additionality requires that EU funds should not be used to save national resources. This principle is difficult to implement because national budgetary priorities often change and it is difficult to estimate how much the member states would spend if there was no EU funding.

Besides the principle of additionality structural costs are characterized by five other guiding principles:

- Concentration. The costs must be geographically concentrated;
- Coherence. The costs must be in the context of the broad development programs drawn up by the EU member states and approved by the EC;
- The Commission, the member states concerned, regional and local authorities, businesses and trade unions must cooperate in spending;
- Monitoring and evaluation. The costs must be monitored and evaluated;
- Consistency and complementarity. The costs must be consistent with the provisions of the Treaties and Community policies such as the single market, CAP and others.

The following recommendations can be made to the future CP:

- Creating a less uniform regulatory framework. There is a clear need for a more strategic programming approach at member state level and for a stronger role of LRAs. It is necessary to change the paradigm from conditional programming to an approach of final determination. The current follow-on principles for conditionality can be a model to follow;

- Ensuring effective and efficient use of resources. LRAs and member states will have to rethink the need to comply with the "industry standard" and focus on meeting needs rather than demand. The main challenge is the design and functioning of the labor market, social policies and education;
- Public-private partnerships and mobilization of private funds and investments;
- Meeting the CP's needs in terms of governance and the territorial dimension. There is a need for a high quality management at LRA level beyond the level of decentralized units. A territorial approach has to be formulated and integrated into CP principles, measuring the effects and identifying their links to policy and budget.

In Bulgaria there was a trend of accelerated absorption of the European funds and of precise planning of the projects. The analyzed period 2007-2015 was characterized by:

- Contracting more funds than the available budget under some operational programs in order to manage the financial risk at the end of the programming period;
- Activities that could not be finalized by the end of 2015 remained at the expense of the beneficiary;
- Increased attention to the quality of control at central and regional level.

The main problems of the management of the European funds in Bulgaria are:

- Irregularities in public procurements which led to the suspension of funding and financial corrections under some operational programs;
- Lack of working capital, which directly affects the pace of progress and the quality of implementation;
- Insufficient exchange of knowledge and experience between managing authorities, beneficiaries and control bodies.

The following lessons can be drawn from the management and absorption of EU funds in Bulgaria for the period 2007-2013:

- It is advisable that the implementation of projects for the new programming period 2014-2020 start as soon as possible;
- Adopt a new approach in the OP Regions for Growth 2014-2020 in order to avoid concentrating funds in major cities, which was typical for the 2007-2013 period;
- Digitalization of the project application process for the new programming period;
- Codification of the legislation on European funds, which led to the adoption of the European Structural and Investment Funds Management Act at the end of 2015.

The results of the empirical analysis of the short-term effects of the European Union funds on the economic growth, employment and unemployment in Bulgaria confirm the importance of the external economic conditions for the short-term economic growth of Bulgaria. This conclusion is in line with the theoretical expectations, as the Bulgarian economy is small in size and with a high degree of openness.

An interesting result of the empirical analysis is that the employment rate in Bulgaria depends only on the employment rate in the previous period. This result could be explained by the inertia of the labor market in Bulgaria and the reproduction of past trends based on adaptive expectations. Evidence to support such an explanation is the lack of influence of the attitudes of business agents and international conditions on employment in Bulgaria.

Unlike the employment rate, the unemployment rate in Bulgaria is affected not only by the value of the indicator in the previous quarter but also by the attitudes of the business agents. The lack of impact of the external economic environment on employment and unemployment in Bulgaria is indicative of inertia, rigidity and difficult adaptation of the

Bulgarian labor market to changes in the economic environment.

It can be concluded that in the short run the absorption of EU funds does not affect economic growth, employment and unemployment in Bulgaria. This means that EU funds cannot be used as a tool for a quick economic recovery from crises.

From the empirical assessment of the impact of the absorption of EU funds on the natural rate of unemployment and the rate of long-term unemployment, the following conclusions can be drawn:

- There is a significant positive relationship between the rate of absorption of EU funds and the rate of long-term unemployment (the natural rate of unemployment), which is contrary to theoretical expectations and could be explained by an increase in structural unemployment resulting from the financing of innovations with EU funds. Such a relationship should be a signal of concern to political and economic strategists at national and European level, as it indicates an adversary impact of the absorbed EU funds on the long-term unemployment rate and the natural rate of unemployment in Bulgaria;
- There is a significant negative relationship between the real GDP growth rate and the long-term unemployment rate (the natural rate of unemployment) that corresponds to theoretical expectations and can be considered a confirmation of the hypothesis of the existence of hysteresis.

The empirical assessment of the impact of the absorbed EU funds on the potential GDP of Bulgaria suggests that while in the short run the absorption of the EU funds does not affect economic growth, employment and unemployment in Bulgaria, in the long term it has a positive effect on potential GDP and total factor productivity, but a negative impact on potential employment and the rate of long-term unemployment. Potential GDP and total factor productivity rise due to improvements in technology and infrastructure, but the quantity and quality of human capital is on decline (the rate of long-term unemployment increases). It is recommended that investment in human capital be raised in order to enhance its quantity and quality and to maximize the beneficial long-term effects of the absorbed EU funds on the Bulgarian economy.

Economic growth is a key objective of macroeconomic policy and a source of the wealth of a nation. The characteristics of economic growth (factors, trends and problems) are influenced by the type of the exchange rate regime of the country. Exchange rate regime is a key factor of macroeconomic management (target and tool of macroeconomic policy) and its characteristics change in terms of regional economic integration. During the integration process the importance of national exchange rate policy gradually decreases and disappears completely when the country joins a currency area. The type of the exchange rate regime has a specific impact on the effectiveness of macroeconomic policies and on the integration of the national economy in economic and monetary unions (Todorov, 2014).

Problems with the growth of the Bulgarian economy are complex and severe. Their successful solution requires a combination of short-term measures to stimulate aggregate demand and long-term measures to impact aggregate supply. Unfortunately, the Bulgarian macroeconomic management lacks rationality and the discussions on the important macroeconomic problems of Bulgaria are led by extreme ideological positions (from an extreme neo-Keynesian activism to a neoliberal market fundamentalism). The formulation and the implementation of an effective macroeconomic policy is not an ideological but a pragmatic problem. A proper macroeconomic policy is neither totally left-wing nor totally right-wing; neither fully neo-Keynesian nor completely neoliberal. A proper macroeconomic policy is pragmatic, functional and workable. It can combine both neo-Keynesian and neoliberal measures; both left-wing and right-wing actions. What is important is to effectively solve the current economic problems of society. It is therefore advisable that experts solve the economic problems without excessive politicizing and ideologizing.

The Bulgarian economy still forms its structural characteristics and seeks to enhance its overall competitiveness. The Bulgarian currency board arrangement successfully maintains financial stability (at least till the case of the Corporate Commercial Bank), but its limitations further worsen the problems with the growth of the Bulgarian economy. It is recommended that as soon as possible Bulgaria enter the Exchange Rate Mechanism 2 (ERM 2), which is a "waiting room" for the euro zone. After a two-year stay in the ERM 2 and after successfully meeting the Maastricht convergence criteria Bulgaria will be able to join the Eurozone. The membership in the Eurozone is expected to bring to Bulgaria the following benefits that can contribute to solving the problems with the growth of the Bulgarian economy:

- The interest rate premium for country risk of Bulgaria ought to drop, which will stimulate the flow of capital (long-term oriented and not speculative!) to Bulgaria and the interest rates in Bulgaria will decrease to levels comparable with those in the Eurozone;
- Restrictions imposed by the currency board on the "lender of last resort" (refinancing of the banking system by the central bank) will be removed;
- There will be no need for Bulgaria to maintain such large foreign exchange reserves and part of the released reserves can be used for other purposes instead of maintaining a fixed exchange rate;
- Exchange rate risk and transaction costs between Bulgaria and the Eurozone will be removed;

- The better access of the Bulgarian National Bank (BNB) to the operations of the European Central Bank (ECB) will provide additional liquidity that can stimulate lending and growth.

Bulgaria fulfils the optimum currency area criteria and the Maastricht criteria even in crisis conditions. The global economic crisis, the ensuing recession and the debt crisis in the Eurozone slowed down the process of real and nominal convergence with several years. Before the global crisis Bulgaria was expected to adopt the euro around 2015. Taking into account the delay in the integration process it is more likely that Bulgaria will join the euro zone at the end of the current decade. The most likely scenario for the adoption of the euro in Bulgaria is a maintenance of the currency board arrangement and an observance of the new imposed by the crisis European requirements.

The specifics of the Bulgarian economy are determined by several factors:

- Size of the economy - small;
- Degree of openness of the economy - high;
- Type of the exchange rate regime - CBA;
- Resource base of the economy - limited;
- Way of integration in the global economy - a current membership in a regional integration union (EU) and a future membership in a monetary union (the Eurozone).

These specific factors dictate macroeconomic policy that complies with the latest European and world realities. Bulgaria's macroeconomic indicators should be maintained around the average for the euro zone to ensure the smooth continuation of the process of nominal and real convergence.

Bulgarian governments conduct a more restrictive fiscal policy than that required by the European standards. Such a policy could harm the growth potential of the Bulgarian economy. Although Bulgaria has registered weak economic growth since 2010, this economic recovery is illusory, because the main growth drivers on the demand side- consumption and investment - stagnate. Only net exports are positive due to the increasing exports of raw materials. With a deficit financial account of the balance of payments, with stagnant consumption and investment the growth forecasts of the Bulgarian economy from the standpoint of aggregate demand are pessimistic.

The analysis of the economic growth in Bulgaria on the supply side shows that Bulgaria cannot rely on an extensive growth by increasing employment for several reasons:

- Decrease of the working-age population due to demographic problems;
- Emigration from the country by young and highly productive workforce;
- Low contribution of employment to economic growth in the period of operation of the CBA.

Changes in capital stock (net investment) and total factor productivity are the main determinants of economic growth in Bulgaria on the supply side. It is therefore advisable to carry out macroeconomic policies that stimulate investment and productivity.

Investment can be stimulated through the following measures on the supply side:

- Improvement of legislation and the work of state institutions, reduction of bureaucracy and corruption;
- Implementation of consistent, predictable and adequate to the European and global realities macroeconomic policy to bring foreign investment back to Bulgaria.

Productivity can be enhanced through the following measures on the supply side:

- An increase in the investment in public infrastructure;
- A rise in the expenditure on human capital formation (education, qualification and training) and in spending on improving the quality of the workforce (healthcare, culture, sports);

- An increase in the investment in research and development.

Possible are also measures aimed at increasing the rate of saving, such as reducing the tax on deposits, as according to the endogenous growth theory the higher saving rate leads to higher investment and higher productivity in the long term.

In Bulgaria the quantity and quality of human capital is low, there is a lack of good public infrastructure, research and development is far from the European standards. Given that investment in public infrastructure, in research and development and in human capital formation as a percentage of GDP in Bulgaria is several times lower than the EU average, the forecasts for long-term growth of the Bulgarian economy can only be pessimistic.

The weak legislation, the poor functioning of state institutions, the high bureaucracy and corruption, the lack of consistency and continuity in the macroeconomic policies of different governments make prospects for growth of the Bulgarian economy from the viewpoint of aggregate supply even worse.

This study on economic growth in Bulgaria has the following similarities with other studies on this issue:

- In terms of the employed methodology (growth accounting) the present research resembles the studies by Ganev (2005), Minassian (2008), Raleva (2013) and Todorov (2015);
- In terms of the indicator used to measure employment (number of hours worked) this research is similar to the study by Raleva (2013);
- In terms of the approach employed to assess the growth of capital stock (constant capital-to-output ratio) this research resembles the studies by Minassian (2008 and 2010), Raleva (2013) and Todorov (2015);
- In terms of the approach used to assess the elasticity coefficients on the basis of the income structure of GDP, the current research is similar to the studies by Ganev (2005), Raleva (2013) and Todorov (2015);

- In terms of the conclusions reached and the results obtained this research and the investigations by Ganev (2005), Minassian (2010), Raleva (2013) and Todorov (2015) are alike.

The OLS procedure results suggest that the first equilibrium approach provides the most accurate and reliable estimates of the elasticities α and β in Bulgaria's aggregate production function. This inference could be explained by two circumstances:

1) The first equilibrium approach is based on the final expenditure structure of Bulgaria's GDP, while the other four equilibrium approaches are based on the income structure of Bulgaria's GDP;
2) The estimation of GDP by the income approach in the official Bulgarian statistics is not reliable because it is obtained post factum, as a residual and reflects only the primary distribution of income and does not take into account the redistribution of income.

The comparison of the results from the two OLS estimations (with annual and quarterly data) and the first equilibrium estimation of Bulgaria's aggregate production function leads to the following conclusions:

- The estimated values of the elasticity of output with respect to capital α via different methods are close or even coincide (the OLS estimator of α is 0.25 with annual data and 0.22 with quarterly data, while the first equilibrium approach generated an average value of 0.22 for the period 1997-2013);
- The estimated values of the elasticity of output with respect to labor β via different methods significantly differ from each other: (an OLS estimator with annual data of 0.99, an OLS estimator with quarterly data of 0.39 and an average of 0.78 by the first equilibrium approach for the period 1997-2013);

- The coefficient α is significant at the 1% level in both OLS procedures (with annual and quarterly data);
- The coefficient β is significant at the 5% level in the OLS procedure with annual data and at the 10% level in the OLS procedure with quarterly data;
- The OLS estimation with annual data indicates increasing returns to scale ($\alpha + \beta = 1.24 > 1$), while the OLS estimation with quarterly data shows decreasing returns to scale ($\alpha + \beta = 0.61 < 1$). However, in both OLS procedures the Wald test confirms the null hypothesis that $\alpha+\beta=1$ at the 5% level of significance. This agrees with the assumption of constant returns to scale of the neoclassical growth theory;
- The intercept A is insignificant in both OLS procedures ((with annual and quarterly data).
- Both OLS estimations should be treated with caution for different reasons: the one with annual data because of the short time series (19 observations) and the other with quarterly data because of spillover effects and seasonal fluctuations.

When growth accounting is applied to Bulgaria, it is recommended that the first equilibrium approach to calculating elasticity coefficients be used.

The results of growth accounting using the first equilibrium approach provide evidence that total factor productivity and capital stock have been the main supply-side determinants of Bulgaria's economic growth under a CBA, while employment has had an insignificant negative impact on growth. This inference implies that Bulgarian policymakers have to concentrate their efforts on encouraging productivity improvement and investment in order to stimulate economic growth.

Labor productivity per person employed and per hour worked in Bulgaria is 30-40% of EU average, which makes Bulgarian workforce the least productive one in the EU (Todorov, 2014).

The experience of Bulgaria and other transition economies has proved that investment activity is determined mainly by institutional and macroeconomic environment, while tax stimuli and other preferences have relatively weaker impact on investors' decisions. In spite of its low corporate tax rate of 10%, Bulgaria has attracted less investment than other transition economies from Central and Eastern Europe with higher corporate tax rates.

Bulgaria's institutional environment is characterized by high levels of bureaucracy and corruption and by sluggish and ineffective work of state administration. The lack of good legislation and quality institutions, the absence of quality infrastructure and the shortage of well-qualified and highly-productive labor force are the main obstacles to investment (local and foreign). Other factors, which impede investment, are the political instability and the absence of succession and continuity in macroeconomic policies of different Bulgarian governments.

Bulgaria may create favorable conditions for increasing productivity and investment by:

1) Improving the quality of its legislation and institutions;
2) Building good public infrastructure;
3) Encouraging and investing in the formation of human capital;
4) Stimulating and investing in research and development (R&D) activities.

Considering the slow and painful process of institutional transformation in Bulgaria, as well as the low share of investment in public infrastructure, human capital and research and development in Bulgaria's GDP compared to EU levels, the supply-side prospects of Bulgaria's economic growth cannot be good.

The present study has some similarities to and some differences from the other investigations in Bulgaria's economic growth in the transition to a market-oriented economy:

- In terms of its first objective (to identify the best equilibrium approach to calculating elasticities in Bulgaria's aggregate production function) the present empirical investigation differs from the previous studies of Bulgaria's economic growth in the transition to a market-oriented economy;
- In terms of the used methodology (a combination of an OLS estimation and five equilibrium approaches to estimating elasticities in the production function) the present empirical investigation differs from the previous studies of Bulgaria's economic growth in the transition to a market-oriented economy;
- In terms of the indicator used to measure employment (the number of employed person) the present research resembles the investigations of Minassian (2008), but differs from the studies of Ganev (2005) and Raleva (2013), where employment was measures by the number of hours worked;
- In terms of the approach used to estimate the growth rate of capital stock (constant capital-output ratio), the present study is similar to the investigations of Minassian (2008) and Raleva (2013), but differs from the research of Ganev (2005), where the growth rate of capital stock was estimated by the perpetual inventory method;
- In terms of the equilibrium approaches used to calculate the elasticity coefficients in the production function, the present research employs and compares five approaches based on both the final expenditure structure and the income structure of GDP. The previous studies about Bulgaria's economic growth use either expenditure-based equilibrium approaches (Minassian, 2008), or income-based equilibrium approaches (Ganev, 2005, Raleva, 2013) but not both.

A contribution of the present study to empirical research into Bulgaria's economic growth is the conclusion that the equilibrium approach based on the final expenditure structure of GDP provides more accurate and reliable estimates of the elasticities α and β in Bulgaria's aggregate production function than the other analyzed four approaches, which are based on the income structure of GDP.

Analyzing and predicting the business cycle is a relatively new part of economic science, which is becoming more and more important to modern economists. Estimating the business cycle phases contributes to the successful forecast of the economic environment. An opportunity is given for the prior compilation of an economic strategy to mitigate upcoming economic shocks or to enhance the impact of expected positive economic policy outcomes.

There are few studies on the Bulgaria's business cycle. Good knowledge of the theoretical formulation of business cycles allows for more in-depth research in this area to the economy of Bulgaria. There is a necessity to increase the efficiency of the economic policy in Bulgaria in the years after the transition. Proper business cycle analysis can provide the answers that Bulgarian macroeconomic strategists need in order to address the economic difficulties faced by the country.

The research results confirm the Keynesian thesis of the disequilibrium character of the economic system. The lack of co-integration among macroeconomic variables indicates the absence of a stable long-term market equilibrium, which makes state intervention in the economy necessary. In case of a permanent and persistent deflationary GDP gap and deflationary trends policymakers should seek a combination of short-term demand-side stimuli and long-run supply-side measures.

The short-term demand-side stimuli ought to be fiscal because fiscal policy is the only macroeconomic instrument available under a currency board arrangement. Bulgaria's governments customarily implement more restrictive policies than European standards require and in this sense opportunities exist to stimulate aggregate demand through fiscal policy. Fiscal solutions ought to be sought in the following directions:

1) Improving the EU funds absorption rate. Considering the low absorption rate of EU funds in Bulgaria (about 30%) there are a lot of reserves in this area;
2) Introducing moderate progressive taxes on corporate profits and personal income. As shown by Tanchev (2016), progressive income taxation has a positive impact on Bulgaria's economic growth, while proportional income taxation has a negative influence on the real GDP of Bulgaria;
3) Lowering the rates of the Value Added Tax and the excise taxes on electricity and other energy sources used for manufacturing purpose. Such a measure aims at reducing production cost and prices and at encouraging consumption and production;
4) Balancing the government budget not by cutting expenditure but by optimizing it and by increasing revenue;
5) Transforming the tax system from a consumption-based one to a hybrid one, which is considered more stimulating to the economic growth (Stoilova, 2017);
6) Increasing the share of budget expenditure in GDP to the Euro area average. Maintaining fiscal parameters close to the Euro area average ought to facilitate the fulfillment of the Maastricht criteria for public finance.

The structures of Bulgaria's state budget have a lot of defects and create multiple problems, which require adequate management solutions. Whether Bulgaria's macroeconomic management possesses the necessary will and competence to find and implement these solutions is difficult to forecast.

The long-run supply-side measures are related to:

1) Improving the quality of legislation and institutions;

2) Building good public infrastructure;
3) Encouraging and investing in the formation of human capital;
4) Stimulating and investing in research and development (R&D) activities.

Bulgaria's institutional environment is characterized by high levels of bureaucracy and corruption and by sluggish and ineffective work of state administration. The lack of good legislation and quality institutions, the absence of quality infrastructure and the shortage of well-qualified and highly-productive labor force are the main obstacles to investment (local and foreign). Other factors, which impede investment, are the political instability and the absence of succession and continuity in macroeconomic policies of different Bulgarian governments.

Considering the slow and painful process of institutional transformation in Bulgaria, as well as the low share of investment in public infrastructure, human capital and research and development in Bulgaria's GDP compared to EU levels, the supply-side prospects of Bulgaria's economic growth cannot be good.

Bulgaria's ineffective money market, which remains much below its equilibrium levels in a period of economic stagnation, indicates the necessity of increasing the money supply in order to stimulate economic growth. A possible way to encourage growth is to improve the efficiency of financial markets in Bulgaria.

REFERENCES

1. Abramovitz, M., 1956. Resource and Output Trends in the United States since 1870. American Economic Review, 46, pp. 5-23.
2. Bachtler, J. and Mendez, C. (2007). Who governs EU Cohesion policy? Deconstructing the reforms of the Structural Funds. Journal of Common Market Studies, Vol. 45, No. 3, pp. 535-564
3. Barca, F. (2009). An Agenda for a reformed Cohesion Policy, A place-based approach to meeting European Union challenges and expectations. April 2009.
4. Boehme et al. (2013). Study on promoting multi-level governance in support of Europe 2020. Inception Report, European Commission Regional and Urban Policy.
5. Burns, A. F. and Mitchell, W. C. (1946). Measuring business cycles. NBER.
6. Carlgren, M. (2015). Comparing turning point predictions for growth cycles. Department of Economics, Umea University.
7. Cassel, G. (1967). The theory of social economy. New York. Augustus M. Kelley. Publishers. p. 538.
8. Christiano, L. J., Eichenbaum, M. and Evans, C. L. (2005). Nominal Rigidities and the Dynamic Effects of a Shock to Monetary Policy. Journal of Political Economy, 113(1), 1-45.
9. Clarida, R., Gali, J. and Gertler, M. (1999). The Science of Monetary Policy: A New Keynesian Perspective. Journal of Economic Literature, 37(4), 1661-1707.
10. Cohesion Policy 2007-13: Commentaries and Official Texts, January 2007, DG Regio.
11. Cororaton, C., 2002. Total Factor Productivity in the Philippines. Philippine Institute for Development Studies Discussion Paper No. 2002-01.

12. De Sismondi, J.-C.-L. S. (1819). Nouveaux Principes d'Economie Politique: Ou de la Richesse dans ses Rapports avec la Population. Delaunay.
13. Denison, E., 1967. Why Growth Rates Differ. Washington: The Brookings Institution.
14. Denison, E., 1985. Trends in American Economic Growth, 1929-1982. Washington: The Brookings Institution.
15. Dougherty, C. and Jorgenson, D., 1996. International Comparisons of the Sources of Economic Growth. American Economic Review, 86(2), pp. 25-29.
16. Economic Research Institute at the Bulgarian Academy of Sciences, 2012. Annual Report 2012 "Economic Development and Policy in Bulgaria: Evaluations and Expectations. Special Focus: Competitiveness of Bulgarian Economy".
17. European Commission (2007). Fourth Report on Economic and Social Cohesion. Office for Official Publications of the European Communities, Luxembourg.
18. European Commission, 2014a. Macroeconomic Imbalances: Bulgaria 2014. Occasional Papers 173, March 2014.
19. European Commission, 2014b. The Production Function Methodology for Calculating Potential Growth Rates & Output Gaps. Economic Papers 535 November 2014.
20. European Commission, 2015. Bulgaria: Report prepared in accordance with Article 126(3) of the Treaty. Brussels, 16.11.2015 COM (2015) 802 final.
21. European Committee of the Regions (2012). The complementarity of national and Community interventions aimed at reducing disparities in economic and social development. Commissioned by Committee of the Regions, DTC Unit 4.

22. European Committee of the Regions (2015a). The Future of Cohesion Policy: Report I.
23. European Committee of the Regions (2015b). The Future of Cohesion Policy: Report II.
24. Felipe, J., 1997. Total Factor Productivity Growth in East Asia: A Critical Survey. Asian Development Bank Working paper.
25. Fischer, S. (1977). Long-term Contracts, Rational Expectations and the Optimal Money Supply Rule. Journal of Political Economy, 85(1), 191-205.
26. Friedman, M. and Schwartz, A. J. (1965). Money and Business Cycles. University of Chicago and NBER.
27. Gali, J. (2008). Monetary Policy, Inflation, and the Business Cycle: An Introduction to the New Keynesian Framework. Princeton University Press. p. 5.
28. Ganchev, G., 2010. The fulfillment of the Maastricht criteria in Bulgaria. In: Bulgaria's accession to the Euro area: economic and social dimensions, pp. 9-31. The Economics and International Relations Institute and the Friedrich Ebert Foundation.
29. Ganev, K. (2005). Measuring Total Factor Productivity: Growth Accounting for Bulgaria. Bulgarian National Bank Discussion Paper No. 48/2005.
30. Ganev, K. (2015). Biznes tsikli: Teorii i modeli. Sofiyski universitet 'Sv. Kliment Ohridski'. Sofiya.
31. Ganev, K., 2004. Statistical estimates of the deviations from the macroeconomic potential. An application to the economy of Bulgaria. Agency for Economic Analysis and Forecasting Working Paper 12004en.
32. Ganev, K., 2005. Measuring Total Factor Productivity: Growth Accounting for Bulgaria. Bulgarian National Bank Discussion Paper No. 48/2005.
33. Ganev, K., 2015. A Small Model for Output Gap and Potential Growth Estimation: An Application to

Bulgaria. St Kliment Ohridski University of Sofia, Faculty of Economics and Business Administration / Center for Economic Theories and Policies Bulgarian Economic Papers Series bep-2015-04.
34. Garvy, G. (1943). Kondratieff's theory of long cycles. NBER. The Review of Economic Statistics, 25(4) p.203-220.
35. Gladnishki, A. (2005). Measuring potential output: using the instruments of production functions. Agency for Economic Analysis and Forecasting (AEAF), Ministry of Finance, Republic of Bulgaria.
36. Hall, R. and Jones, C., 1996. The Productivity of Nations. National Bureau of Economic Research Working Paper No. 5812.
37. Hayek, F. A. (1935[1931]). Prices and Production. Augustus M. Kelly, Publishers, New York.
38. Hernandez, J. A. and Mauleon, I., 2003. Estimating the Capital Stock. Working paper, Universidad de la Laguna; Universidad de Las Palmas de Gran Canaria.
39. http://ec.europa.eu/eurostat
40. http://www.nsi.bg/
41. https://eumis2020.government.bg/
42. https://www.eufunds.bg/izpalnenie-na-operativnite-programi
43. International Monetary Fund, 2010. Bulgaria: Selected Issues. IMF Country Report No. 10/159, June 2010.
44. International Monetary Fund, 2014. Bulgaria's EU Funds Absorption: Maximizing the Potential. IMF Working Paper WP/14/21.
45. Jevons, W. S. (1884). Investigations in Currency and Finance. London. Macmillan and Co.
46. Juglar, C. (1862). Des crises commerciales et leur retour périodique en France, en Angleterre, et aux Etats-Unis. Guillaumin et Cie.

47. Kacharnazov, N., 2008. The Model IS-LM as a Research Method for Economic Fluctuations of Bulgarian Economy. Dialog 2/2008.
48. Keppel, C. and A. Orthofer, 2009. A macroeconomic forecasting model for Bulgaria.
49. Keyns, Dzh. M. (1993). Obshta teoriya na zaetostta, lihvata i parite. izd. 'Hristo Botev', Sofiya.
50. Kitchin, J. (1923). 'Cycles and trends in economic factors'. Review of Economics and Statistics. 5 (1): p.10–16.
51. Kondratieff, N. D. (1935). The long waves in economic Life. The Review of Economics and Statistics. 17(6) p. 105–115.
52. KPMJ (2016). EU Funds in Central and Eastern Europe. Progress Report 2007-2015.
53. Krueger, A., 1999. Measuring Labor's Share. National Bureau of Economic Research Working Paper No. 7006.
54. Kuznets, S. (1929). Random events and cyclical oscillations. Journal of the American Statistical Association, 24 (167), 258-275.
55. Kuznets, S. (1930). Secular movements in production and prices. Their nature and their bearing upon cyclical fluctuations. Boston: Houghton Mifflin.
56. Kuznets, S. (1971). Modern economic growth: Findings and reflections, Lecture to the memory of Alfred Nobel, December 11, p. 1.
57. Kydland, F. E., and Prescott, E. C. (1988). The Workweek of Capital and Its Cyclical Implications. Journal of Monetary Economics, 21, 343-360.
58. Lucas, R. E. (1973). Some International Evidence on Output-Inflation Tradeoffs. American Economic Review, 63(3), 326-334.
59. Maddison, A., 1982. Phases of Capitalist Development. Oxford: Oxford University Press.

60. Malthus, T. (1798). An Essay on the Principle of Population. An Essay on the Principle of Population, as it Affects the Future Improvement of Society with Remarks on the Speculations of Mr. Godwin, M. Condorcet, and Other Writers. London: J. Johnson. Electronic Scholarly Publishing. p. 4.
61. Mankiw, G., Romer, D. and Weil, D. N., 1992. A Contribution to the Empirics of Economic growth. Quarterly Journal of Economics 107(2), pp. 407–437.
62. Manzella, G. P. and Mendez, C. (2009). The turning points of EU Cohesion policy. Report Working Paper, January 2009.
63. Mills, J. (1868). On Credit Cycles, and the Origin of Commercial Panics. In Transactions of the Manchester Statistical Society, pp 9-40.
64. Minassian, G., 2008. Is the Bulgarian Economy Overheating? Economic Thought Journal, 2008(3), pp. 3-29 (in Bulgarian).
65. Ministry of Finance of the Republic of Bulgaria, 2014a. Bulgaria's economy 2013: an annual survey. ISSN 2367-5012.
66. Ministry of Finance of the Republic of Bulgaria, 2014b. Medium term budget forecast for the 2015-2017 period.
67. Mirwaldt, K., McMaster, I. and Bachtler, J. (2009). Reconsidering Cohesion Policy: The Contested Debate on Territorial Cohesion. European Policy Research Papers, No. 66, European Policies Research Centre, University of Strathclyde, Glasgow.
68. Mises, L. (1953). The Theory of Money and Credit. Yale University Press. p. 365 – 366.
69. Moore, H. L. (1914). Economic Cycles: Their Law and Cause. Macmillan Pigou, A. C. (1923). Industrial Fluctuations. Macmillan.

70. Naidenova, P. and Mihova, G., 2010. Population Ageing - The Challenge of the New Century. Economics and Management, 2010(3), pp. 2-11 (in Bulgarian).
71. Patonov, N., 2013. Searching for a restraint on the European Leviathan. Scientific Annals of the "Alexandru Ioan Cuza" University of Iasi. Economic Sciences, 60(2), pp. 315-330.
72. Pirimova, V., 2001. Growth, cyclic recurrence, conjuncture. Sofia: Publishing Complex of the University of National and World Economy (in Bulgarian).
73. Pirimova, V., 2014. Cyclic recurrence in the economy: forms, sources, mechanisms. Sofia: Publishing Complex of the University of National and World Economy (in Bulgarian).
74. Raleva, S., 2013. Inflation and Economic Growth. Sofia: Publishing Complex of the University of National and World Economy (in Bulgarian).
75. Schumpeter, J. (1939). Business cycles. A theoretical, historical and statistical analysis of the capitalist process. New York. McGraw-Hill Book Company.
76. Senhadji, A., 2000. Sources of Economic Growth: An Extensive Growth Accounting Exercise. IMF Staff Papers 47(1).
77. Solow, R., 1957. Technical Change and the Aggregate Production Function. Review of Economics and Statistics, 39, pp. 312-320.
78. Statev, S., 2009. Financial development and economic growth. Sofia: Publishing Complex of the University of National and World Economy (in Bulgarian).
79. Stoilova, D. and Patonov, N., 2013. An empirical evidence for the impact of taxation on economy growth in the European Union. Tourism and Management

Studies, 2013(3), pp. 1030–1033, http://tmstudies.net/index.php/ectms/article/view/485

80. Stoilova, D., 2007. Fostering Local Development in Bulgaria: The Need of Fiscal Decentralization. In: Local Innovations for Growth in Central and Eastern Europe. Paris: OECD Publishing, 277-292, DOI: http://dx.doi.org/10.1787/9789264038523-15-en.
81. Stoilova, D., 2010. Financial Decentralization and the Downturn: Evidence from Bulgaria. Scientific Annals of the "Alexandru Ioan Cuza" University of Iasi, Economic Sciences Section, LVII, pp. 261-275.
82. Stoilova, D., 2017. Tax Structure and Economic Growth: Evidence from the European Union. Contaduria y Administracion, Volume 62, Issue 4.
83. Tanchev, S. 2016. The Role of the Proportional Income Tax on Economic Growth of Bulgaria. Economic Studies journal, Volume 2016, Issue 4, pp. 66-77.
84. Todorov, I. (2016). Supply-Side Factors of Economic Growth in Bulgaria. Economic Alternatives, Issue 2, pp. 159-174.
85. Todorov, I. (2017). The Growth and the Cyclical Recurrence of Bulgaria's Economy under a Currency Board Arrangement. Sofia: Avangard Prima.
86. Todorov, I. and K. Durova (2016). Economic Growth of Bulgaria and Its Determinants. Economic Studies journal, Volume 2016, Issue 4, pp. 3-35.
87. Todorov, I., 2014. Exchange-Rate Regimes on the Path to Euro. Economic Studies Journal, 2014(1), pp. 116-147 (in Bulgarian).
88. Todorov, I., 2014. Macroeconomic trends in the new member countries of the European Union before the Euro Area debt crisis. Analele Stiintifice ale Universitatii Al I Cuza din Iasi - Sectiunea Stiinte Economice, 61(2), pp. 197-217.

89. Todorov, I., 2015. Two Approaches for Evaluating the Aggregated Production Function of Bulgaria. Economic Studies Journal, 2015(4), pp. 67-81 (in Bulgarian).
90. Todorov, Iv. (2016). Makroikonomika. Izd. Avangard Prima. Sofiya.
91. Tsalinski, T., 2007. Two Approaches to Estimating the Potential Output of Bulgaria. Bulgarian National Bank Discussion Paper No. 57/2007.
92. Wicksell, K. (1953[1907]). The Enigma of Business Cycles. International Economic Papers, 3, p. 224.
93. World Bank. 2005. Bulgaria: The Road to Successful EU Integration. The Policy Agenda. Country Economic Memorandum. Report No. 34233-BG.

Bei Fragen zur Produktsicherheit wenden Sie sich bitte an:
If you have any questions regarding product safety,
please contact:

Walter de Gruyter GmbH
Genthiner Straße 13
10785 Berlin
productsafety@degruyterbrill.com